Appalachian Safari

Appalachian Safari

A Virginia Mountain Man's Wild Stories

David Adam Atwell

AuthorHouse™
1663 Liberty Drive
Bloomington, IN 47403
www.authorhouse.com
Phone: 1-800-839-8640

© 2013 by David Adam Atwell. All rights reserved.

No part of this book may be reproduced, stored in a retrieval system, or transmitted by any means without the written permission of the author.

Published by AuthorHouse   02/15/2013

ISBN: 978-1-4817-1329-0 (sc)
ISBN: 978-1-4817-1328-3 (hc)
ISBN: 978-1-4817-1327-6 (e)

Library of Congress Control Number: 2013902311

Any people depicted in stock imagery provided by Thinkstock are models, and such images are being used for illustrative purposes only.
Certain stock imagery © Thinkstock.

This book is printed on acid-free paper.

Because of the dynamic nature of the Internet, any web addresses or links contained in this book may have changed since publication and may no longer be valid. The views expressed in this work are solely those of the author and do not necessarily reflect the views of the publisher, and the publisher hereby disclaims any responsibility for them.

For my son, Wyatt.

Thank you Amy for all your love and support; and for taking some of the photographs in this book.

Thank you dad for teaching me not to sweat the small stuff; and for editing this book.

Table of Contents

Table of Photographs .... *ix*

Prologue .... *xi*

1. *My First Deer* *1*
2. *The First Day of Trout Season* *5*
3. *Aim Small Miss Small* *9*
4. *Instinct Shooting My First Turkey* *15*
5. *Getting Shot by a Friend* *17*
6. *Rabbits are Easier to Hit than Deer* *19*
7. *Hiking and Camping in the U.S. Army* *21*
8. *Unbelievable Skill with a Muzzleloader* *27*
9. *Goin' Up Cripple Creek* *31*
10. *Screaming Eagle* *33*
11. *Everyone Eventually Gets Turned Around in the Woods* *37*
12. *Canoeing Bull Run in Manassas* *41*
13. *Hiking and Climbing the German Alps* *45*
14. *Hunting Cabins* *53*
15. *Which is more important, the shooter or the rifle?* *59*
16. *Army Marksmanship* *61*

17.	Oh Crappie! 67
18.	My First Spring Gobbler 69
19.	Catfishing 71
20.	My Best Friend 75
21.	Hunting the Great American Buffalo 80
22.	Staying Warm in a Hunting Blind 87
23.	Trekkin' and Pickin' with the Old Grey Owl 91
24.	When Deer Attack! 93
25.	Sailing on the Potomac River 95
26.	Naming My Son Wyatt 99
27.	Where are the Bear Hunting Stories? 101
28.	GPS, Land, & Celestial Navigation 103
29.	Makin' Moonshine 109
30.	The Family Truck Tradition 111
Epilogue 113

Table of Photographs

Photo 1: The Farm, looking north from the base of the south ridge. (Prologue) .... *xiii*

Photo 2: My First Deer, a 10 Point buck, barely. (Chapter 1)......*4*

Photo 3: Aim Small Miss Small Shooting Target. (Chapter 3)....*14*

Photo 4: My Suzuki Samurai with a canoe on top. (Chapter 12)....*42*

Photo 5: The observation deck of the Zugspitze, that's me on the left. (Chapter 13) *51*

Photo 6: My best friend and wife, Amy. (Chapter 20)................*77*

Photo 7: A sketch of The Bison Ranch at Couteau Ridge (Chapter 21) *84*

Photo 8: The possibles bag and powder horn made from my buffalo. (Chapter 21) *86*

Photo 9: Staying warm in a hunting blind. (Chapter 22)............*89*

Photo 10: Sailing my micro-cruiser with my sister Annie. (Chapter 25) *97*

Prologue

Suddenly realizing I had most likely reached the midpoint of my life at age 37, a sense of pride and sadness overwhelmed me in the winter of 2011-2012. I had accomplished so much in my life, shared it with so many great people, but still felt that I had a lot to do before my time on Earth ends. Specifically, the lifelong dream of writing a book had eluded me even though I had tried writing one numerous times about various topics. This goal regularly haunted my thoughts, but something felt very different that day. I felt that I had a greater purpose driving me and a shining example to follow.

It is truly amazing what can inspire a person to take action, in this case an 18 year old young lady I had never met and a 3 year old boy. Selena McGrady, a student of my home town high school, had published her first book earlier in 2011 at age 18. A work of fiction in the fantasy genre named the "The Wizard's War". I became aware of her work when reading my hometown newspaper on the Internet and instantly ordered two copies, a traditional paperback for my bookshelf and an electronic version (eBook) for my iPad. The novel took just a couple days to read, about 260 pages, and I enjoyed every page. I am looking forward to her future works. Most importantly, I had a great sense of pride that a young lady from my hometown, and still in high school no less, had successfully gotten her book written, published, and available for sale on Amazon.com and the Apple iBook store. I thought, "If she can do it, I can too!" So, I got to work and reached out to her publisher.

The 3 year old boy who also inspired this book could be considered a more traditional source of inspiration, he is my son. My wife and I only have one child and like most parents we believe the sun rises and sets over his head. Like most fathers I want Wyatt to follow in my footsteps, have the same experiences I had as a child, and grow up to be a strong, handsome, courteous, generous, humble, and successful man. My wife and I spend time with him every day trying to teach him about the most important things in life, but I often wonder if I will be around long enough to complete the lessons. After all, I still learn from my father whenever I spend time with him, but my mother passed away when I was only 18 years old. Therein lies the motivation for writing this book, it's an opportunity to continue the lessons after I am gone and share them with future generations of the family.

Before you continue with the rest of this book there are some things you need to know. First and foremost, all these stories are true, they actually happened, but like most camping, fishing, shooting, and hunting stories poetic license has been used to make the stories more interesting, funny, teach a lesson, or to protect the identity of some unknowing, unwilling, and extremely humorous participants. Secondly, some of the stories took place at a relatively unknown place that my family calls, "The Farm".

The farm consists of about 50 acres of unbroken mountain farmland in a small valley between two steep ridges in the Blue Ridge Mountains of southwest Virginia. The general area is referred to by locals as Dutton Valley and is near the town of Rural Retreat nestled in the New River Valley.

The small valley between the two ridges of the farm consists of an open field, a creek, and two springs. One of my uncles, Dewey, dug out the eastern most spring in the 1990s to make a small trout pond. The south ridge is so steep that a man can hardly stand up straight without tumbling down it. Bushes and a few small trees cover the south ridge and the creek runs along its base. The valley slowly rises from the base of the south ridge towards the north ridge with a couple saddles joining the field with the forest at the bottom edge of the north ridge.

The north ridge is steep, but not as steep as the south ridge; you can walk up it and stand up straight, but would have a hard time getting a vehicle up it, even a four wheel drive. We know this because my other uncle, Mike (Mike Sr.) and Paw Paw, Estle, once dented a truck tailgate and bumper pretty bad by rolling backwards off the north ridge right into a tree! Unfortunately, this became a family tradition, but you will have to keep reading this book to find out how.

Photo 1: The Farm, looking north from the base of the south ridge.

Half way between the two ridges were some fruit trees, a great big pear tree and a few smaller apple trees. We used to keep a hog pen near the eastern spring (long before the pond existed) and a small tobacco field in the southwest corner of the farm. The last two things you need to know about the farm include "The Pine Tree", and the "Milk Barn". The Pine Tree is rooted in the northeast corner of the farm, almost at the top of the north ridge. It's an old large pine tree that sits between two great deer trails; my family has been hunting out of that tree for about four generations.

The tree is so large and tall you can easily see it from a distance any time of year. Sitting in that pine tree on a cold crisp fall or winter morning you can faintly hear the train whistles blow in town. The Milk Barn is located in the southeast corner of the farm at the foot of the south ridge and next to the creek, about a half a mile away from the pine tree. It's a cinder block building about the size of a large garden shed or a one car garage and has 2 stalls for milking cows. It still stands today.

    The farm is somewhat isolated because of the winding gravel road and steep ridges that make up the only way into the hollar. For example, when my father and I used to work the farm as dairy men (OK, dairy man and dairy boy) the tanker trucks that pick up farmers' milk and deliver it to the milk plant could not navigate the roads and steep ridges, so we had to milk our dozen cows into old fashioned milk cans twice a day and haul the milk out to a milk tank in town ourselves so the dairy trucks could pick up our milk. That was in the early 1980s and the roads have not changed a bit. Another good example of the farm's isolation is that when phone and electrical lines were installed at the farm new cables and poles had to be ran for about a mile and over the steep south ridge just to connect one house. Today there are only 3 houses using those lines.

    Now that you have an adequate understanding of this book's genesis and a backdrop for the stories you are probably wondering about the title "Appalachian Safari". The stories in this book are all about hiking, camping, hunting, fishing, and observing animals (including manimals) in their natural habitat, a safari, an Appalachian Safari!

Chapter 1

My First Deer

Running down the north ridge of the farm towards the milk barn with my heart pounding and only one thought in my head I slammed into the barn's cinder block wall and then ran around to the front. I had to find my dad! I yanked open the door and looked inside expecting to see him right there where we had camped the night before, but he was gone. I sort of remembered seeing a truck on top the hill on the west side of the farm as I crossed the valley; so I backed up, looked up the hill to my left, and confirmed the existence of the truck. I knew my dad liked that area because he could see the entire farm from an elevated position, giving himself an excellent opportunity at any deer that happened to leave the safety of the tree line. There's a corner fence post that makes a great gun rest and a natural contour in the ground that makes a good seat. Having a young body and strong heart of only 13 years I didn't even realize or care that I had just run about a half mile down the north ridge, across the valley (north to south), and was about to start another half mile run westward across the valley and uphill to my dad.

I arrived on top of the hill huffing and puffing to find my father excited and laughing. I guess the sight of his son running about a mile as fast as he could and taking the long way around to boot was more than he could bear that morning. I blurted out, "I got one!", and my dad grew more excited. I said, "He has antlers like this!" and placed both hands above my head with all my fingers spread apart. My father could no longer control himself and said, "Come on, let's go!" We joined our cousin Bronson at his truck, drove across the farm, and up the north ridge as far as we dared. On the way we realized that I had probably shot the deer Bronson had taken a shot at about an hour earlier when he and my dad had run the ridge for me. Running a ridge is when one group of hunters walk a ridge hoping to flush game towards another group of hunters.

    We jumped out of the truck, ran up the rest of the ridge, and I showed them where the buck laid. They instantly started picking on me because I had lain my shotgun down across the body of the buck and then placed some brush over the deer so no one would steal it. They said, while smiling, "What happened? Did you shoot it while it's horns were hung up in that brush?" Quickly realizing that my story would not improve the situation, I didn't even try to explain that I had tried to hide the deer from potential thieves. Instead, I just started telling them everything that had happened that morning.

    My fingers and toes hurt from the cold, it was about 9:30 AM and I usually gave up hunting by that time, choosing a warm fire and hot tea instead of battling the elements. However, on that sunny November morning in 1987, sitting in the pine tree my family had hunted from for years, I told myself to wait just a little longer. A few more minutes went by, and PAH-KOOOOOO, I heard a shot! I also heard a deer running through the woods just west of me, but couldn't see it. I stood up in the tree stand and held my shotgun ready; a Stevens single barrel hinge action 12 gauge that my Paw Paw had given me. I saw movement, about 75 yards out to the west. The deer ran up towards the top of the ridge and stopped at the crest about 100 yards west and uphill from me. I could see the sun glinting off his antlers and remember thinking, "A very nice rack, he might even be an 8 pointer!" while hoping he would run in my direction. The buck turned left, then right, and ran straight towards me! I cocked the hammer of my shotgun, raised it to my shoulder and waited. The deer had to run at least 80 yards before I could get a good shot. I picked a spot between two trees and decided that when the deer ran behind those trees

I would shoot him in the gap between the trees. This placed the deer somewhere between 20 and 25 yards from me and perfectly broadside.

Heart pounding, I waited, waited, and slapped the trigger! BOOM! The buck flipped over sideways, away from me, and never moved again. 00 Buckshot is lethal at 20 to 25 yards. I could barely contain myself, but knew I had to wait in the tree stand for at least 15 - 20 minutes to allow the deer to pass on in peace. The last thing we both needed was an adrenaline crazed romp through the brush. You already know what happened next; I had to find my dad!

The buck's atypical rack officially had 10 points, yep, my fist deer was a 10 pointer, but the last two points were questionable. At barely an inch long you could hang a ring off those last two points, as long as the rack did not move and gravity cooperated. Good or bad, this buck set the tone for deer hunting the rest of my life. On the good side, I thoroughly enjoy deer hunting and do not feel any pressure or need to harvest big bucks, hunt just for sport, or to compete with family and friends. However, on the bad side I had already taken a 10 point buck and had top notch bragging rights at age 13. Where do you go from there? For the real irony, just look at the following picture of the deer's antlers. Yes, I still have the rack, it's the only set of horns I ever mounted on a board, and I rarely show them off.

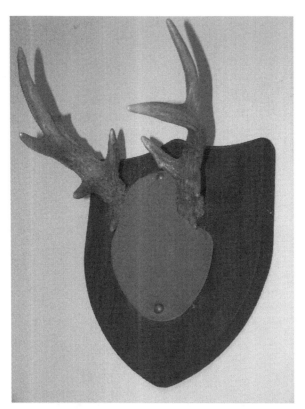

Photo 2: My first deer, a 10 point buck, barely.

Chapter 2

The First Day of Trout Season

The most nostalgic memory from my youth involves a fishing tradition that disappeared as the unintended consequence of a very successful wildlife management and a productive fish hatchery program in the Commonwealth of Virginia. Current and future generations of anglers enjoy practically unrestricted fishing access to stocked trout waters year round in Virginia, but it wasn't always so. Trout fishing used to have a limited season. The Department of Game and Inland Fisheries (DGIF) publishes a schedule of which creeks and ponds will be stocked with trout, continues to establish reasonable creel limits, sells a trout stamp authorizing licensed anglers to fish for trout any time of year, and the proceeds from the trout stamp goes towards the cost of hatching, raising, and stocking the trout. Never since European settlers first set foot in Virginia and fished for the native brookies has trout fishing been so readily accessible and easy to do. However, lost to us all is the anticipation, thrill, and excitement of the opening day of trout season.

    Sitting on the ground near the water's edge of the "Big Pond" in Crawfish Valley I could feel the excitement in the air as about 100 men, women, and children busied themselves all around the pond preparing their fishing tackle and waiting for trout season to officially open. The forestry service, DGIF, and volunteers always kept the area around the pond well maintained, and on opening day we could always expect well cut grass, nice gravel trails, and a shoreline absent of any downed trees from the winter. Wherever stocked trout waters flowed through the commonwealth the same scene played out that morning, the opening day of trout season. People lined creek banks as far as the eye could see and sat or stood shoulder to shoulder around ponds. Some arrived before daylight to claim their favorite fishing spots, some camped out the night before, and others came running up at the last minute hoping to squeeze in wherever they could. My dad and I had claimed a great spot on the damn of the "Big Pond" near the water overflow; we fished on the dam every year. The "Big Pond" is one of two ponds located close to each other in the Wythe County section of the Jefferson National Forest. The other pond, obviously named the "Little Pond" due to its relative size, rested just a few hundred yards away down a hill and through the woods. My Uncle Mike preferred to fish the "Little Pond", but sometimes fished the shallow end of the "Big Pond" from the bed of creek rocks where the stream flowed into it.

  A cool breeze blew across the pond rippling the glass surface and causing me to shiver, so I stuck my hands in the large front pocket of my red pull over hoodie to keep them warm, and waited. People around us debated who would catch their limit first and how long it would take. They debated the best bait to use this year; red wigglers, corn, pink salmon eggs, orange salmon eggs, or a rooster tail. However, no one got upset, raised their voice, or argued over a fishing spot. We were all happy to be there that early spring morning after a long winter of snowy and cold weather. Suddenly, the Game Warden, or a self-appointed time keeper, gave the signal and simultaneously about 100 fishing poles rose in the air casting bait, hook, line, and sinker towards the center of the pond. The entire scene resembled a well-choreographed show put on by a group of synchronized swimmers.

  The hatchery raised trout didn't take long to start biting, after a few minutes you would start to see a few people jerking their fishing poles to set a hook. Watching closely and paying attention you could also start to see a pattern as a school of trout obviously swam around the pond causing a small ripple of pole jerking through the crowd, similar to a group of football fans doing the wave at a stadium. After a couple hours dad and I would have our limit, 6 trout each, or we would have had enough of fishing for the day and head home.

    The trip home always involved a few stops; one to check in with Uncle Mike and brag about our catch, another to see my Paw Paw to do the same, and a stop at a country store to get a Dr. Pepper and a Reese's Cup. Once we arrived at home my dad wasted no time, he fired up the grill or warmed up the oven. We cleaned the trout, placed butter and cajun spices inside them, and wrapped them in tin foil. The trout baked until the skin could be easily peeled back with a fork and the meat lifted lightly off the bones in chunks. I don't eat a lot of fish, but to this day very few foods are better than fresh cajun spiced trout caught and cooked the same day.

    A few years ago my wife and I went camping down Crawfish Valley near the ponds with my Uncle Mike's family. I decided to take my wife fishing up at the "Big Pond" and felt a great sense of sadness when we arrived. Fallen trees blocked most of the parking area, the trails leading up to the pond were overgrown, and downed trees made most of the shoreline hard to fish. Obviously, no large crowds of hundreds of people had fished the "Big Pond" in years. Year round trout fishing and government budget cuts had taken their toll. The DGIF does offer a couple programs that provide a similar experience to the opening day of trout season, but they just aren't the same. The urban trout fishing program stocks ponds and creeks near urban and suburban areas and the first fishing day after stocking usually draws a small crowd. The free fishing days in June also draw small crowds to ponds and lakes in established parks all over the Commonwealth.

Chapter 3

Aim Small Miss Small

People usually look at me strange when I tell them I learned to shoot at age 5. I assume they do not believe me or do not think it's possible or appropriate for a 5 year old child to learn to shot. The truth is that I really learned to shot at age 3, but I quit telling people that years ago because the conversations never went well. My family considers marksmanship an important skill to learn and an American tradition; unlike some families my sisters even learned to shoot.

My first shooting lessons involved a plastic double barrel toy shotgun that shot suction cup darts. It came with a wind up plastic rabbit that would "run" across the floor so you could try to shoot it. I think my dad enjoyed that gun more than I did; however, I have to honestly admit that I have fuzzy memories about the gun but remember the rabbit quite vividly. My son's first shooting lessons have involved a Daisy "Buck" BB gun shooting at an 8.5"x11" piece of paper at 5 yards and a Nerf double-barrel shotgun that shoots suction cup foam darts. We usually shoot the BB gun over at the Fairfax Rod & Gun Club from a bench rest position and the Nerf shotgun at home standing or sitting in the family room. Sometimes I even roll a ball across the floor for him to shoot at with the shotgun. The BB gun and the Nerf shotgun have already allowed Wyatt, at age 3, to learn these fundamentals.

1. *Always keep the muzzle, the part of the gun that barks and bites, pointed away from people (and the dogs).*

2. *Always keep your finger off the trigger.*

3. *Basic Positions and Grip for a long gun.*

4. *Hand and Eye Coordination necessary to instinctively hit a reasonably sized target, such as a sheet of paper or 9" ball at 5 yards.*

5. *How to safely load and unload a hinge action firearm (good thing I keep all my guns and ammo locked up).*

My father claims he had me shooting nickels with a daisy BB gun at age 5, but I seem to remember dimes instead of nickels. He would flip a coin in the air and I would take a shot with my BB gun, but mostly I just remember thinking it's impossible. He would tell me to just raise the gun the same way every time and look at the coin. Evidently, I would hit a few of them, but most importantly I can remember the excitement of my dad hitting more than he missed whenever he demonstrated how to do it. Shooting at very small targets became a theme with us. While my cousins, friends, and their fathers were shooting at old plastic milk jugs and 2-liter soda bottles my dad had us shooting at milk jug lids and soda bottle caps. I even remember my dad setting up an indoor BB gun range for me one winter and having me shoot at very small bullseyes. Aim small miss small was our mantra.

My dad made it clear that I always needed to concentrate when shooting, shoot at small targets, keep the sites aligned, minimize movement of the rifle, hold my breath when I shoot, squeeze the trigger, and follow through. Aiming at a very small target actually made all of these things easier to accomplish, and if I aimed at a small target and missed it, I found that I would only miss by a small distance. This meant that when shooting with my friends I could aim at an imaginary dot in the center of the milk jugs and 2-liter soda bottles, and actually hit many more targets than my friends. This also worked out really well in the long run too because when hunting, or shooting in the Army, the targets don't have bullseyes to help you aim.

I clearly remember one specific shooting lesson back at the farm in the northwest corner by one of the springs. I was 14 years old and shooting at a target on a fence post about 25 yards away with my new .30-30 rifle using iron sights. I wasn't allowed to have a scope unless I earned enough money to pay for it myself. I started to develop a flinch because of the recoil and remember closing my eyes, jerking the trigger, and just hoping it didn't hurt too bad each time I fired. Unfortunately, all my father saw was me missing the target and the rifle muzzle moving significantly off target just before each shot. He explained, numerous times, that I needed to quit jerking the trigger and shouldn't move the rifle just before I shoot because an inch of movement at the muzzle of the barrel would cause me to miss the target by a foot or more. The more I shot the more frustrated he became and my shooting just got worse.

Looking back I believe we had reached the limit of both my shooting ability at the time and my dad's ability to teach me about shooting. You have to keep in mind that my dad, like most fathers, was not a trained, certified, or licensed firearms or marksmanship instructor. He was just a man, teaching his son to shoot the same way he had been taught to shoot. Unfortunately, shortly after that event my interest in shooting waned, but it probably had as much to do with puberty, girls, and high school as with that specific day of shooting.

Living in the mostly suburban region of Northern Virginia at age 22 and shortly after my discharge from the Army in 1996 I started missing the fun of shooting and hunting and decided to take it up again. By 2001 and age 27, I had become a National Rifle Association (NRA) Certified Firearms Instructor and a Virginia Hunter Education Instructor. I also quickly formed my own training company, BBSG Academy, to respond to the demand for firearms training after the 9/11 attacks. The "BBSG" stood for "Becoming Better and Safer with Guns". I also started volunteering my time as a 4-H Shooting Coach. Working with certified and experienced instructors and mentoring thousands of new shooters improved my marksmanship and taught me a few things about teaching new shooters.

- ✓ *Make sure the gun size, weight, and caliber match the abilities of the shooter, and use light loads to reduce recoil.*

- ✓ *Use a target large enough and/or close enough for the shooter to be successful.*

- ✓ *Provide positive reinforcement after missed shots by pointing out something the shooter did well.*

- ✓ *Instead of telling the shooter what they did wrong, such as jerking the trigger; tell them what they need to do right, such as gently pressing the trigger.*

- ✓ *Watch the shooter instead of the target, because you should be identifying and correcting bad technique. You can look at the target after the shot is fired.*

- ✓ *At the end of each training session, stop shooting on a positive note before the shooter has exceeded his/her ability and starts to become exhausted and/or frustrated.*

So, how did I reconcile what I learned as a trained and certified instructor with my family tradition of Aim Small Miss Small? Easily, the only real difference between the two methods is a little bit of teaching technique and the size of the targets. As a certified firearms instructor I incorporated my father's approach of concentrating on the fundamentals and using small targets by developing a BBSG Academy target that was simultaneously large enough to easily hit and small enough to teach the Aim Small Miss Small tradition. This innovation allowed new shooters to stay motivated longer and concentrate on the fundamentals of marksmanship instead of worrying about whether or not they hit the target. The target consists of two concentric bullseyes centered on an 8.5"x11" piece of paper and is designed to be shot at 25', but can also be shot at 50' or 75' (25 yards). The primary bullseye is a black or white 1" circle and the secondary bullseye is a grey, white, or black 3" circle. Obviously, the 1" bullseye is in the center of the 3" bullseye. There are no numbers in the circles for scoring, but a simple rating key is printed on the target; Center Dot=Excellent, Circle=Great, and On the Paper=Good. This simple rating system lets a new shooter know just how well they are doing. They aim for and try to hit the small bullseye, but as long as they hit the paper they are doing well.

How can I make such an outrageous claim? Someone shooting at a 1" circle at 25' and misses it, but still hits the paper, is a good shooter?!? That's what the tradition of aim small miss small is all about! Remember, all I had to do with my friends was hit the plastic milk jug or soda bottle. However, as a marksman I personally tried to hit the imaginary dot in the center of the jug/bottle. In early American shooting competitions our forefathers tried to hit the center of an X where the two lines crossed or tried to shoot the flame off a candle without hitting the candle because almost anyone could easily hit a larger target!

Furthermore, keep in mind the real purpose of shooting. Most people own a firearm for self-defense or hunting. In either situation the vital area that includes the heart and lungs is the target, depending on the type and size of the animal this area could be a circle anywhere from 1" to 9" in diameter. The target described above focuses on that 1" to 9" goal, plus the target and bullseyes are realistic because they are proportional and can be used for teaching both pistol and rifle marksmanship. Someone who can hit the 1" circle at 25 feet can probably hit the 3" circle at 25 yards (75 feet) and will definitely hit the paper at that distance. A person who can hit the paper at 25 yards has the technical marksmanship skills necessary to defend themselves or harvest a big game animal at 25 yards. Plus, if they can hit the 1" or 3" circle at 25 yards they can probably easily hit the paper up to 100 yards away with a rifle!

Once Wyatt can hit the rolling ball with his Nerf shotgun I'll start throwing it in the air and eventually replace it with smaller balls; plus when he understands how to use the sights on his BB gun he'll start aiming for that small 1" bullseye too. I just hope he enjoys shooting as much as his Paw Paw and I. Now I just need to teach him how to play chess, but that's another story.

A printable "Aim Small Miss Small" target in PDF format is available for download at the Appalachian Safari website and Facebook page.

http://www.appalachiansafari.com/

http://www.facebook.com/myappalachiansafari

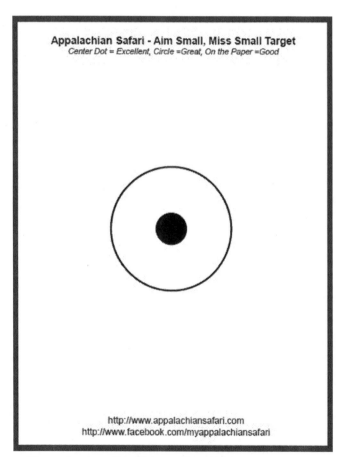

Photo 3: Aim Small Miss Small Shooting Target.

Chapter 4

Instinct Shooting My First Turkey

Before starting this story let me make perfectly clear that "Stalking and Instinct Shooting" and "Walking through the Woods Swinging on Game" are two completely different things. Stalking and instinct shooting can be done safely and are excellent tools for a hunter, but require practice, mentoring, self-discipline, and attention to detail. However, swinging on game is a dangerous unsafe act that has gotten people killed and severely hurt in the woods; hunters should never react to the unexpected appearance or sound of game by simply turning and shooting (like an idiot).

* * * * *

Slowly stalking my way up the northwest side of a draw on the farm east of ours, approaching what we called the "Twin Trees", I came across a flock of turkeys. About a dozen and half of them scratching around for food near the top of the ridge on the opposite side of the draw from me, about 30 yards away. Before leaving the house I had checked the game laws and knew that turkeys were still in season, so I contemplated whether to take a turkey and call it a day or continue hunting for the deer I had been tracking. Looking back, this should have been a "no brainer"; the birds hadn't seen me yet and it was a safe and easy shot.

Without warning, the birds made the decision for me! In a tornado of flapping wings and feathers the entire flock started running and took flight. I must have made a noise or maybe they just saw me. I picked out a big one running to my right at about 2 o'clock and started to raise my gun. As the stock touched my cheek the turkey took flight and I fired! The turkey tumbled about 3 feet to the ground and started flopping all over the place. By the time I made my way across the draw the turkey had quit moving. I tagged it, grabbed it by the feet, and proudly started walking towards camp to show my Uncle Mike.

Chapter 5

Getting Shot by a Friend

The moral of this story is obvious from the title, be careful who you take hunting and shooting. I had a couple of close friends in the summer of 1986 and we were all about 11 or 12 years old. They walked over to my house a lot because I had to stay home and help my mom take care of my sisters. One bright summer day standing in the driveway where my dad usually parked his car we decided to go shooting. I ran in the house to grab a few guns, one for each of us, and let my mother know I would be out for a while. "One, two, and three, that should do it." I counted as I grabbed 3 rifles off my bedroom wall, "Mom, I'm goin' shootin'!"

I dashed out the front door and down the steps. In the driveway, I handed Bubba a rifle and the other guy a rifle. Bubba cocked his gun, pointed it right at my belly, and pulled the trigger. I instantly felt a sharp pain, lifted my shirt, and saw a BB lodged in my skin with a red ring around it. I reached down and flicked the BB off my belly, grabbed Bubba's BB gun, and yanked it out of his hands yelling, "Why the hell did you shoot me!?!" He staggered backwards and faintly muttered those infamous words, "I thought it was unloaded." I took the other guy's gun back and told them both to go home.

Luckily, I survived and didn't even need a band aid, but I never told my mom and dad what happened. Also, "Bubba" was not the boys real name of course, but I thought it fit. Sorry if your name is Bubba, I mean no disrespect. What scares me now about the entire situation is how lucky I was; I could have just as easily grabbed a .22 LR rifle and handed it to Bubba. However, I knew my dad would have expected us to take the BB guns without him there, so that's what I did. I now keep all my firearms unloaded and locked in a safe with a combination lock.

Chapter 6

Rabbits are Easier to Hit than Deer

Scouting around the farm with my bow I came across a fork in a game trail and planned to take the uphill path when I noticed a rabbit hopping across the downhill trail that led out into the field. About 10 yards away, the rabbit must have saw me too because he stopped and froze, right in the middle of the trail. Having already nocked an arrow, I slowly raised my bow and drew the string back to my anchor point. I loosed the arrow and the rabbit squealed once as the arrow ran him through; but it was a clean shot and he didn't suffer. I field dressed the rabbit and placed him in my coat pocket, turned back around, and headed uphill.

The next 45 minutes or so were uneventful, with me just looking for fresh deer sign and scanning the woods around me. I took a break near the top of the west side of the north ridge, opposite of the "Pine Tree", and had a snack. As usual, I took care to pick a good resting spot beside a tree as big around as me with the tree between me and the area where I thought a deer might come. Assuming I was lucky enough to have one walk up on me, and as luck would have it, about the time I finished my snack I heard a sound. Chaaaa, Chaaaa, Chaaaa, Chaaaa; the sound of a deer walking through the forest.

A doe topped the ridge from the opposite side and started walking down the draw in front of me towards the open field. She crossed about 15 yards directly ahead of me and gracefully ducked under the arrow I shot at her. Standing there in shock, with my rabbit in my pocket, I decided that rabbits were definitely easier to hit than deer.

Chapter 7

Hiking and Camping in the U.S. Army

     I spent 4 years serving in the U.S. Army, have a lot of great memories, and very few bad ones. I never saw combat and like most soldiers who never see combat sometimes feel like I missed out on something; but the truth that I have learned from my Paw Paw, Great Uncle Perry, and other combat veterans is that most, if not all, soldiers who do see combat usually wish they never had. My worst memory is losing a company commander during a training exercise in Germany; and for the conspiracy theorists out there, yes, it really was a training accident. My best memory involved an all day long company sponsored bus trip to the Munich Oktoberfest.

     In the Army we called hiking and camping trips "Field Training Exercises" or FTX for short. Most deployable military units conduct a FTX once or twice per year and the combat units are almost always conducting a FTX somewhere. The deployable Military Intelligence unit I served in overseas went on FTX once a year and what made the field exercises so much fun was the people. As a software analyst in the Army I served as part of the Signal Corp which mostly consists of a bunch of computer programmers, computer operators, cabling & phone technicians, radio operators, and other communications technicians. Since my unit was the operations company of the operations battalion supporting a military intelligence brigade we also worked with a bunch of linguists and intelligence analysts specializing in foreign nations and cultures. In short, most of the people who went on FTX with us were recruited by the Army for their brains and not their brawn or woodsmanship.

 A little known fact about the Army is that most of the recruits come from the southeastern states, Virginia south and Texas east. This means you can expect to have a lot of "good ol'" country boys and girls in any unit. However, the units I served with overseas had a lot of people from the rest of the country and quite a few of them had never shot a rifle or been camping before joining the Army. Hopefully, this will help you understand how the events I am about to relay to you could actually occur.

 Bouncing around in a HMMWV, commonly known as a HUMVEE or Hummer, scouting out the location for our upcoming FTX with the company commander (CO), First Sergeant (Top), and the Training Sergeant I couldn't believe they had asked me along. As a Specialist (SPC/E4) it was highly unusual, but they wanted me and my battle buddy, Ruly, to setup a land navigation course because we had the expertise necessary to do it. After looking at a couple sites the CO chose one adjacent to some fields and a very thick forest that also offered easy access to the trail we planned to follow back to base as part of a 15 kilometer march at the end of the FTX.

 The FTX officially started with a packing list distributed to the entire company by the Executive Officer (XO) while the CO was on TDY (Temporary Duty), which is military jargon for business travel. The extensively thorough packing list included almost every piece of TA-50 (camping and field equipment) issued to us. Having spent most of my weekends hiking or climbing in the Alps since settling into life in Bavaria (southern Germany), I realized the ridiculousness of the packing list and recommended to the XO and Top that it be rewritten because all the gear wasn't necessary and wouldn't fit into our rucksacks. After a few days of no change and no feedback I decided to take matters into my own hands, stuffed everything I could into my rucksack, strapped and taped everything else on the list to the outside of the backpack, and headed to Top's office. I placed the 100+ pound rucksack on the floor outside Top's door where he couldn't see it, knocked politely, and asked if he had a minute. Top nodded, so I grabbed the ruck, took two steps into his office, and dramatically dropped it on the floor in front of his desk. Cool as cucumber, Top looked at the rucksack, looked at me, and said, "OK Atwell, I'll talk to the XO, and the CO when he returns from TDY". We had a new and more realistic packing list within a week.

    Shortly after arriving at the FTX site with the rest of the company, my battle buddy and I setup up our tent using our Army issued shelter halves and then started setting up the land navigation course. The goal of a land navigation course is to provide soldiers with practical experience navigating a team or squad size group of 4-16 soldiers through an unknown area using a map and compass. Each soldier is supposed to know their own pace, the number of steps in 10 yards or 10 meters, and keep track of the distance they have travelled by counting their steps; one person is usually assigned as the official pace keeper for the group, another to handle the map, and one to work the compass. The official standard for using a compass is accuracy in shooting an azimuth within 3-5 degrees, so when Ruly and I setup the land navigation course we made sure to place 2 markers at each destination point, a real one and a fake one about 10 degrees off the real point. The hardest point on this particular course included walking a distance of 1.5 kilometers, blocked by a pond that had to be navigated around, and included an additional fake marker 100 meters directly beyond the true marker.

    We gave each team their list of grid points, bearings, and distances and sent them out on the course the following morning. The young soldiers that Ruly and I had trained during "Sergeant's Time" training over the past year came back with most of the correct markers from the points and the soldiers that hadn't been trained to our standard of dedication and attention to detail came back with more of the fake markers. However, we achieved our mission by midafternoon, everyone had some practical experience navigating in the field and we had reminded them all that just because you come to a place that looks like the right place doesn't mean you have actually reached your destination. A 5 degree or

100 meter mistake using a map and compass can get people killed on a battlefield.

Having completed our mission of establishing a land navigation course and running the company through it a half day ahead of schedule Ruly and I retired to our camp site. By this time, 2 days into the FTX, our area looked like a home away from home. Keep in mind that when we bought mountain climbing gear to use on the weekends we avoided the typically bright colors available and tried to buy everything in shades of black, brown, and green so we could use it to replace equivalent parts of our TA-50. We had self-inflating therma-rest sleeping mats instead of the army issue sleeping pads, goose down sleeping bags instead of the army issue chicken feather ones, a candle lantern to hang up inside our tent, and small hammocks. It was an unusually warm fall day, so we stripped out of our BDUs, camouflage basic duty uniforms, wore only our brown polypropylene thermal underwear (they look like pajamas), put on our our black hiking sandals, and climbed into our hammocks. We made sure to replace our kevlar helmets with our duty baseball caps; after all, a soldier is required to wear headgear outdoors.

After reading and talking for a while we had some visitors, a few Sergeants came over to play cards, talk, and warn us that Top better not catch us hanging out like this, in our "pajamas" and hammocks. About the time they prepared to leave, Top walked right up into the middle of us all. Ruly and I jumped out of our hammocks and landed in the parade rest position! Top bellowed, "Atwell, what the hell are you guys doing?" I informed Top that the land navigation course completed early and included a brief summary of everyone's performance. He looked at each of us, cocked his head sideways at a slight angle and said, "OK, carry on, but don't let the CO catch you guys like this, at least put your pants and boots back on." and walked away.

The last morning of the FTX Top walked around to every tent informing everyone to start breaking camp, when he unsnapped our flap and stuck his head in the tent his glasses fogged up. We were laying inside the warm tent with the candle lantern hanging from the ceiling and playing cards. Top took a deep breath and yelled, "Damn it boys, this ain't no camping trip, break this shit down, and get ready to march 15 klicks, we're rolling out in less than an hour".

    The Training Sergeant had scouted the trail we planned to march and assured the CO a HUMVEE could follow us all the way back to the base, so we had arranged for a vehicle to follow us as a first aid station and to also transport anyone who could not make the entire ruck march. Things started out well and spirits were high, then the trail started to narrow. Eventually, the HUMVEE couldn't even follow us and the CO had to send it around to find a place where the trail crossed a road so the driver could meet up with us later. I remember the CO looking at the Training Sergeant and saying, not asking, "Are you sure you rode your mountain bike all the way up this trail back to the base." The sergeant's response was inaudible. At one point the trail got so close to the river's edge that we had to hold on to trees to keep the weight of our rucksacks from pulling us into the river.

    About 7 klicks into the march we halted, the company had gotten spread out and some soldiers felt unable to continue, mostly the females (but not all of them, some were actually doing better than some of the men). The CO made the decision that the weaker soldiers would not have to carry their ruck sacks the rest of the way. Unfortunately, we did not leave their rucks behind. A few of us had to strap our M-16 rifles onto our own rucksacks, then pick up the abandoned rucks and carry them on our chest by turning them around backwards and placing the straps over our shoulders from front to back. Since there was no HUMVEE to transport the exhausted soldiers we all continued on and after a couple more klicks came to a four lane highway. The CO stopped the column again, on the side of the road, and radioed the HUMVEE. About an hour later a convoy of trucks arrived, the CO called off the rest of the ruck march, and we all rode back to the base. I'm just glad the two rucksacks I carried that day weren't 100+ pounds each.

* * * * *

    The ruck march in this story represents the first time I ever really questioned my future in the U.S. Army. There's an old Army saying, you train like you fight and you fight like you train. I no longer felt confident about going into combat with my peers in the Signal Corps and Military Intelligence. Years later, I realized that had I enlisted as an Airborne Ranger at age 17 and received a $10,000 signing bonus, instead of enlisting as a Software Analyst with no bonus, I probably would have made a career out of the Army and had a very different life. However, as I write this story in 2012 with 20 years of experience in the computer industry, 4 of which were in the U.S. Army, I am confident I made the right decision.

Chapter 8

Unbelievable Skill with a Muzzleloader

My father once shot a deer square between the eyes with a black powder muzzleloading rifle at 150 yards. He is a humble man, but was proud of that shot and the rifle he used to make it; a modern replica of a Virginia Mountain Rifle, similar to a Kentucky Rifle but shorter and without the stock running the full length of the barrel. The percussion rifle also had peep sites, which in combination with my father's skill, made the shot possible. My muzzleloader does not have peep sites, but I once used it to make a shot just as unbelievable as my fathers.

The shot occurred one fall morning while hunting from my Uncle Mike's tree house at the top of the draw that leads up the north ridge to the west most corner of our farm. Yes, I called it a tree house because it was much too large and comfortable to be called a tree stand. Large enough to actually walk around in, or for 2 people to hunt in, the tree stand had a large seat and a small table built into it. Plus, it had waist high wooden walls! I sat in the tree house that morning drinking hot tea from my thermos trying to stay awake; all I was missing was a recliner. The deer, a 6 point buck, originally approached me from the west.

I readied myself as the deer came towards me by cocking the muzzleloader and bringing it up to my shoulder. The deer path he walked on curved down the ridge and around me so I waited until the buck was broadside to me, aimed, and squeezed the trigger. PHUHK. The primer went off, but the powder charge didn't fire! The deer started running so I made a grunting sound from deep in my throat while I re-primed my rifle and the deer slowed to a walk. The deer was now to the east of me and walking slowly; I took aim and fired again. The gun went off that time, but the deer quickly and easily ran out of site. I reloaded and waited. Just in case I had hit him I needed to give the buck some time to settle down before I went to look for a blood trail.

In less than 10 minutes the buck came walking back towards me, this time from the east on the same trail I had once missed a doe on with my bow. I prepared for another shot, the deer turned up the ridge which presented another broadside target, this one at about 75 yards. So, I aimed and squeezed the trigger again, and missed again. As if mocking me, the deer didn't even start to run this time. I reloaded my rifle for the third time and prepared to shoot yet again. The buck had made his way to the top of the ridge by now and at a distance of only 50 yards I felt confident I would hit him this time.

I aimed at an imaginary point in the center of where the deer's heart and lungs should have been and squeezed the trigger. The gun went off again and as the smoke started to clear I saw the buck jump as if he had been hit, but I remember thinking, "Boy, that deer sure did jump funny."

The buck ran the last few steps over the top of the ridge and disappeared down the other side. Having to wait for a little while I decided to reload my rifle. I poured the powder charge down the barrel, started the ball, and then reached for my ramrod. It was gone! I reached for it again then figured out I must have dropped it during the excitement when I reloaded the last time and started looking around on the ground beneath me. Slowly, I started to realize why that deer had jumped funny. I couldn't believe it; 1) I had shot my ramrod and 2) I actually hit a 6 point buck with it! I couldn't decide whether to laugh, cry, or be proud.

I climbed down the tree stand and walked up the draw to where the buck had stood when I hit him. I couldn't find any blood or hair. I looked for about 30 minutes, all around where the deer had stood. Finally, I saw something shiny, walked over, and picked it up. It was a lead ball and the brass tip of my ramrod perfectly fused together, very close to where the deer had stood. I found very little hair and no blood. I broadened my search and looked for another hour, but never found any blood. The best I can figure is that my ramrod had turned upwards during flight or been flipping end over end. Either way, when it struck the deer it must have been vertical instead of horizontal! The slap of that ramrod against the deer's side, near the hind quarters, would explain the lack of blood, finding the ball and tip of my ramrod, and why the deer had jumped funny with his hind legs and rear end rising up and moving away from me while his front legs stayed on the ground. Like I said, my shot was just as unbelievable as my dad's, and I didn't even need peep sites.

Chapter 9

Goin' Up Cripple Creek

My favorite type of fishing is wading ankle to waste deep down a creek anywhere from 5' to 30' across. You catch a lot of perch and sunfish, but depending upon the location of the creek you can also catch trout, redeye (rock bass), smallmouth bass, largemouth bass, horny head suckers, and chubs (suckers without horny heads). Some of these fish can grow to a couple pounds or more in a creek, and creek fish fight a lot harder than pond or lake fish. The ultra-light tackle used in creek fishing also makes it a lot of fun. I've tried fly fishing and found it limiting, even with a sideways rolling cast you still can't get to some of the best areas of a backwoods overgrown mountain stream. I prefer to use a regular ultra-lite rod and reel with rooster tail spinners, flip tail grubs, and rebel crawdads. If you cast all three of those in a creek and don't catch anything you might as well go home, because the fish ain't bitin'!

    My dad and his friend J.D. took me on my first creek fishing experience up Hogback hollow in Reed Creek. I thoroughly enjoyed myself even though I spent most of the day following them up the creek constantly wading from side to side untangling my line from various bushes, overhanging limbs, and submerged rocks. Even with all of that trouble learning to cast in a confined space, I still managed to catch a few fish. One time I fished down Reed Creek in Hogback with my sister Annie, dad, and my wife Amy and we must have caught 40 fish each. Unless it's trout, and they weren't, we usually just catch and release because we don't eat a lot of fish. The last time I went fishing in Hogback it was with my dad and Amy and we fished upstream the same way dad, J.D., and I did on that first fishing trip.

I've also waded and fished the notorious Cripple Creek with my sister Kelly, Bull Run River in the Manassas Battlefield (it's really just a creek), parts of the New River, Holston River, James River, Rappahannock River, Potomac River, and both the north and south forks of the Shenandoah River. However, the place I fish the most now is called Broad Run. Surprisingly, I have caught a little bit of everything in this creek near Bull Run Mountain; mostly big old chubs about a pound or pound and a half, but occasionally a large mouth or small mouth bass too.

There is a small perch native to the creeks on the Piedmont of Virginia that are plentiful enough to be considered the redeye's counterpart in the low lands. This perch doesn't have red eyes, but is similar in size to Rock Bass and you catch a lot of them. I call them crap fish (or shit fish) because they have a mouth like a crappie and every time you catch one they fight so hard that you think you have a much larger fish on the line, but once you lift them out of the water you think, "Oh, shit, another crappie fish."

I once fished down Broad Run with my friend Gator and caught about 40 chubs and shit fish within 100 yards of the bridge we started at before he ever caught a single one. In his defense, Gator had fished ponds and lakes most of his life and was using the wrong kind of lures. It took me an hour to convince him to take one of my one-eighth ounce white rooster tails with a silver spinner, but once he put it on his line he started catching as many fish as me. The next time I fished Broad Run I slipped on some rocks and broke one of my fingers, it was probably karma for picking on Gator so much that day.

When my son is ready, I'll take him fishing down both Bull Run and Broad Run, and when he gets older we might even fish Reed Creek up Hogback holler.

Chapter 10

Screaming Eagle

I remember the day my mother gave me my Indian name, Screaming Eagle, and told me my spirit animal was the Eagle. When I told my dad, he just looked at me, chuckled, and said "Yep, that's about right". Evidently, as a child I talked a lot and was fiercely independent. I also vividly remember the day my mother gave me my first medicine bag to wear around my neck and taught me about tomahawks. Looking back I may have placed too much significance on those events, but I am a spiritual person by nature and have no trouble believing the Native Americans' Great Spirit is the same God I know from the bible and learned about during my Lutheran catechism classes.

Celebrating and studying Native American culture intertwined with the early years of my life. My elementary and high school mascot was an Indian; and as a Virginian, learning the story of Jamestown, Captain John Smith, and Pocahontas was mandatory in school. My family also camped out on the Cherokee Reservation in North Carolina every summer and my father eventually started selling some of his Native American craftwork at a couple shops on the reservation. My father and his friends used to comb the corn fields along the creeks and streams each spring when the farmers started plowing. They were looking for Native American relics and almost always found a few. Arrowheads, drills, and scrapers were common, but occasionally they would find the head of a tomahawk or part of a pipe.

I occasionally joined them on their little expeditions and we eventually became members of the Reed Creek Archeological Society and started participating in formal excavations and the mapping of known Native American village sites. We had a lot of fun each fall and late summer after the farmers' harvest, digging in our 5'x'5 plots uncovering fire pits, post holes from wigwams and the palisade, and occasionally a burial site. Any uncovered relics and remains were photographed, logged, and if appropriate carbon dated. The society allowed us to keep any relics we found, but human remains obviously had to be reburied. The archeological society also conducted a monthly meeting with guest speakers from other chapters, dig sites, and local colleges.

As I learned to hunt, fish, and trap I also learned to respect the animals I harvested by making sure they did not suffer and only taking animals I intended to eat. I learned to respect the land by always taking out more trash and garbage than I carried into the woods, up a mountain, or down a stream. I even learned to instinctively shoot a bow. As I got older I started tanning animal hides into leather, both with the fur on and fur off. My mother taught me to sew the hides and other materials into clothes and how to make beadwork using a loom. Ultimately, as you will read later, I even went on a Buffalo hunt in North Dakota.

My dad makes bone tools and stone tools using traditional methods. He specifically made a significant effort to learn to knap, even though my mother used to say he was already well practiced at napping. Flint knapping is an endangered art form in America, there are probably only a few hundred people left that can use a deer antler to fashion a piece of flint into an arrowhead, drill, knife blade, or other useful tool. After years of practice my dad became one of them, although he eventually switched to knapping stained glass because it was easier to work and cheaper to procure. Plus it was commercially more viable, meaning that he could get stain glass scraps for free and more easily knap them into prettier arrowheads. Whenever asked by a potential buyer whether or not his arrowheads were real, my father always gave the same stock answer, "They're real arrowheads, just not real old"; which I am sure left many a yankee traveling south on I-77 or I-81 with a smile or puzzled look on their face.

My dad honed his craft while working at a reconstructed Indian village in Bland County Virginia that is a living museum, just off I-77. The name of the place is the Wolf Creek Indian Village. My dad worked there for years and my sister, Annie, also worked there for a while. As reenactors, their job consisted of building the village's palisade, building and tearing down wigwams, making baskets, tanning animal hides, and demonstrating other daily tasks from early Native American life for tourists and elementary school kids. I know that for both of them their time working together at the Indian village was very special, but I'm glad I never had to skin a deer that the game department or department of transportation brought in from local car accidents on hot summer days.

In my entire life I have only saw 5 bald eagles in the wild, but the sighting of each punctuated a significant time or change in my life. I saw the first eagle while driving down I-95 from Manassas to Richmond to personally oversee my first major project as an Information Technology (IT) manager. Crossing the Rappahannock River I looked up and saw the eagle soaring 20 feet above me, hundreds of feet above the river. I took it as a good omen. The second eagle appeared along the Potomac as I rode a train into Washington, D.C. from Manassas to start a new management job with a Fortune 500 company. I actually saw this eagle many times while riding the train to work, but only count it as one sighting. I also believe this may have been one of the two famous eagles known along the upper Potomac at that time as George and Martha.

The third and fourth bald eagles I saw swooping down on their prey on the same day, about 5 miles apart. I was visiting the Northern Neck of Virginia, a peninsula on the Chesapeake Bay between the Potomac and Rappahannock rivers, and had just met with the board of directors of a beach, boating, camping, and hunting club I had recently joined and also learned about a once in a lifetime opportunity to buy two small pieces of land along the Potomac River on a short sell for an unbelievable price. After seeing those two eagles, I obviously did whatever was necessary to buy that land.

    Just this past summer (2011), Wyatt and I both saw the fifth bald eagle together while fishing Cotting Lake at Fairfax Rod & Gun Club. The eagle swooped down, grabbed a fish out of the lake, and flew away. I can't help but wonder, maybe my mother was right after all.

Chapter 11

Everyone Eventually Gets Turned Around in the Woods

My first significant overnight hiking trip consisted of a three day youth group Llama Trek on Mount Rogers, the highest mountain in Virginia, and taught me a valuable lesson about keeping your bearings in the woods. One of the leaders and I became mighty confused about our location a couple times, but thankfully never really got lost. We left camp to fetch water from the spring the first day, and without our map had a little trouble finding our way back to camp. The next day we were hiking at the back of the group and talking so much that when we looked up the rest of the group was nowhere to be seen. We had to back track several hundred yards and take a different fork in the trail to catch back up with everyone. Since that trip I have committed myself to paying attention to my surroundings, using maps extensively, and not getting lost in the woods. I later expanded that commitment to include not getting lost on the water when I took up sailing.

I once owned property and a hunting cabin in northern Virginia on top of Blue Mountain. The property bordered the G.R. Thompson Wildlife Management Area, nearly 4,000 acres of public hunting land near Front Royal and Linden. After hunting the surrounding area for a few years I decided to start inviting some friends to join me. However, keep in mind that after being shot by a friend with a BB gun in my youth I had become very picky about the people I shoot and hunt with, so the people I invited were usually soldiers, veterans, firearms instructors, or other hunter education instructors. One friend, an Air Force Veteran, and I decided to go deer hunting one weekend after a wet snow. In case you don't know this, a wet snow tends to cause fog, especially in the mountains.

After settling into the cabin my friend and I decided to scout around a little bit even though a thick fog limited visibility to just a couple hundred yards. I wanted to investigate a small depression about a mile into the woods that I thought would be a good place to hunt. No game trails led towards the depression from the cabin, but I knew the terrain well and easily guided us in the right direction. We crossed under a power line, walked a few hundred yards more, and arrived about 100 yards to the right of depression. I took note of an unusually large oak tree with a much thinner fallen tree leaned against it as my landmark for navigating back to the cabin and we walked over to the depression. Unfortunately, hidden from my observation another tree had also fallen against the opposite side of the large oak.

We scouted around for a while and eventually decided not to hunt the depression and started making our way back to the cabin. By this time the fog and woods had reduced visibility to less than 100 yards, but we used the big oak tree with the smaller tree leaning against it to make our way back to the cabin. After a few hundred yards I became worried that we hadn't crossed under the power line and recommended we make our way back to the oak tree to get our bearings and start again. We realized our mistake this time because we noticed both leaning trees. Adjusting our heading based on the original leaning tree we started out again, but by now visibility had dropped to less than 50 yards. We made it to the power line and kept walking.

The second power line perplexed me. I couldn't remember ever coming across a second power line. Realizing that something had to be wrong I recommended we follow the power line for a while, and about two hundred yards down the line we came across a large flat rock that I recognized. I instantly knew what had happened, only one power line existed and we had walked in a circle back to the same power line in the fog! We started laughing, which relieved the knot that had started to grow in my stomach, took a new heading off the rock, and were drinking coffee and tea in the cabin within an hour.

Chapter 12

Canoeing Bull Run in Manassas

While stationed at Fort Myers in Arlington, Virginia I met and started dating my wife, Amy. We spent a lot of time camping and canoeing in the Shenandoah Valley and outskirts of Northern Virginia. One of our first canoeing trips started at the Stone Bridge just off Route 29 and wound through Bull Run Park down to Route 28. We left my black Ford pickup truck down at 28 and hauled the canoe up to 29 on top of my small Suzuki Samurai sport utility vehicle. People had to think we were crazy; the canoe was easily twice as long as the Samurai.

Floating down Bull Run, Amy made fun of my accent because I kept saying paddle on the right or paddle on the left, but it sounded like pedal on the right and pedal on the left. Then she brought up that she had never understood if I meant color or collar whenever I talked about my shirts; evidently I tend to say both words the same way. Otherwise, things were going well until we reached the first major bend in river. Now keep in mind that even though people call Bull Run a river it is only about 30 feet across, and we were in a 14 foot canoe. When we reached the bend neither one of us paddled hard enough and we ended up getting slammed into a tree trunk in the corner of the bend. Making matters worse we starting taking on water over the side of the canoe and flipped it right there in the strongest part of the current. I came out of the water on the upstream side of the canoe laughing, but Amy was not as lucky. She came up on the downstream side wedged between the canoe and the tree. She was up and talking so it took me a few seconds to realize Amy needed help. The water was only about 4 feet deep and gently pushing me into the canoe, but the canoe was pushing her into the tree. Finally realizing Amy's predicament, I helped free her from the canoe's watery vice. We righted the canoe, climbed back in, and laughed together as we noticed a family having a picnic on bank of the river and staring at us like we were idiots.

Photo 4: My Suzuki Samurai with a canoe on top

Later that summer my baby sister, Kelly, came to visit us for a week. I guess I shouldn't call her my baby sister because she was probably 15 or 16 at the time and she's now a grown woman and mother of two wonderful boys. However, she's my youngest sister, 8 years my junior, and will always be the baby of the family. Plus, I know referring to her as my baby sister will aggravate her, and as a good brother it's my obligation to both torment and assist my sisters whenever possible. Anyway, Kelly came up to visit and we all three decided to go canoeing down Bull Run. We loaded up the canoe on the Samurai and parked the Ford truck down by 28 again. The first half of the trip was uneventful.

About half way or maybe three quarters of the way between routes 29 and 28 another creek joins Bull Run, the river banks become a little steeper, and the water tends to stay a little muddier. Typically, you cannot see the bottom in this area and this is exactly where my sister decided to display her Atwell temper. I forget the topic of conversation, but remember clearly that Kelly didn't like the way the discussion was going and decided to demonstrate her displeasure by throwing here paddle overboard. Sitting in the middle of the canoe, she placed her hands on her hips and stared at me defiantly. I stared right back and in a mocking tone said, "Way to go moron, now you have to go get it." Without missing a beat Kelly leaped over the side of the canoe and started walking towards the paddle then simply disappeared. A second later she popped back up and grasped the side of the canoe in a panic. Evidently, the current from both streams had cut a deep channel in that part of the river and Kelly had stepped right off a shelf into it. After safely hauling Kelly back up into the canoe, without tipping over I might add, we managed to recover her paddle and had a good laugh the rest of the way down the river.

Chapter 13

Hiking and Climbing the German Alps

The wind cut like a razor and snow blew so thick we couldn't see more than 100 meters (about 110 yards) in any direction. The weather had gotten worse after we left the protection of the cliff wall and rock out croppings to make our way up the long, and exposed, switch backs to the last camp before making our summit attempt the next day. We knew we were close to the Knorrhutte (Knorr Cabin) and hoped to make it there before the visibility got any worse and forced us to spend the night in our emergency bivy bags. We slowly started to make out a dark shape in the white wall above us as the hutte began to materialize. When we neared the hutte the cabin master came out to greet us, "Gruess Gott!, he exclaimed. We responded in kind, "Gruess Gott!" a traditional Bavarian greeting that literally means "God's Greetings".

Sitting inside the wonderfully warm Knorr Hutte enjoying bergsteigeressen and getrank (Mountain Climber's Meal and Drink) we all marveled at the unusual weather that June. Anytime you climb above 6,000 feet you have to prepare for any type of weather, year round, but no one really expects to end up in a freak blizzard in the early summer. The cabin master informed us the hutte and trail were closing because of the weather and we would have to go back down the mountain in the morning. We had lost our chance to make the summit! We were disappointed, but also knew we could try again later that summer. The Zugspitze might be the highest mountain in Germany, but it isn't the hardest to climb.

While stationed overseas in Augsburg, Germany, about an hour northwest of Munich, I spent most of my weekends and free time hiking, climbing, or skiing in the mountains. I enjoyed Garmisch-Partenkirchen the most, but also spent some time in Berchtesgaden. These two cities hosted the two highest peaks in Germany, the Zugspitze and the Watzmann. The Zugspitze stood just under 10,000 feet at 2,962 meters and the Watzmann was 2,713 meters. While there was only two ways up the Watzmann there were a half dozen ways up the Zugspitze. I took a cog train up the Zugspitze the first time and a gigantic cable car the second time. A cog train is a small local line train with a center rail and sprocket that prevents the train from slipping down on the rails. The Zugspitze has a glacier on top that allows skiing to take place late into the summer; the glacier, in combination with the its height, make the Zugspitze quite a tourist destination. Even though I went up the Zugspitze five times those were the only two times I did it the easy way. The northeast face of the Zugspitze is a traditional climb, but has been climbed for so long that steel cables and ladders make it more accessible. I preferred hiking and climbing the back side of the mountain because it was easier and more beautiful.

I never actually made it to the top of the Watzmann even though I tried twice. The weather just never cooperated with us, it's a shame too because a lot of people have told me that climbing the Watzmann makes you feel like you are on the moon because once you reach the summit all you can see, as far as you can see, is a rocky landscape. However, I did hike up to the Eagle's Nest to get a look at Adolf Hitler's mountain retreat once. I can understand why he liked the place; the view was breath taking even though it was a cloudy day. The thick low level clouds looked like the ocean below me and all the mountain tops looked like a group of islands nestled in the water.

Almost all my Garmisch hiking and climbing trips originated at the Olympia Skistadion, the stadium that hosted the 1936 Winter Olympics just prior to World War II. The summer games were held in Berlin that year and ironically the 1940 Olympic Games were scheduled to be hosted by Japan but got cancelled. However, one spring weekend my climbing partner Jeff and I decided to do something different and climb the Kramerspitz on the north side of Garmicsh. We walked up the first mile of mountain on a paved path until we reached the St. Martin hutte, which was really a restaurant, and then the trail became a normal mountain trail. As we got about half way up the mountain we started to hear small avalanches falling above us, which obviously started to make us a little nervous. We knew we were a little early in the season, but thought it would be safe, so we kept on going. We eventually came to a switch back on the trail that had a small bridge across a narrow ravine and were surprised to find the bridge gone and avalanche debris clogging the ravine. We decided to eat lunch and ponder our situation. After a cold lunch of summer sausage and cheese with a beautiful view of Garmisch below and the Zugspitze across the valley we decided to take out our ice axes, rope up, and cross the ravine. Jeff setup as belay and I started across. I made it about half way when an old German man came around the next switchback, walking down the trail, and whistling. He stopped where the bridge had been, looked at both of us, and then walked right across the packed snow filling the ravine. Jeff and I looked at each other in stunned silence for a few minutes and decided that neither one of us needed to be on the mountain that day. We hiked back down to the St. Martin hutte and surprisingly found them open. We walked into the cabin, warmed up by the fire, ordered Wiener Schnitzel mit Pommes Frites (fried pork filet with french fries), and had a beer. It turned out to be opening day for the hutte and we were their first customers of the year. That was the largest and best piece of Weiner Schnitzel I have ever had in my life. By time we made it back down to Jeff's car the weather had changed to sheets of rain and I am sure a couple thousand feet up the snow was probably blowing hard.

    Jeff and I took some Army buddies and hiked up into the Oberreintal bowl once, it's a climbers paradise with vertical cliff walls 200-300 meters tall all the way around 360 degrees, except the narrow mouth where we entered the bowl. This trip started like most others at the olympic stadium and through the Partnachklamm gorge, but about a third of the way up the valley to the Zugspitze we took a left and went up an extremely vertical trail with switch backs every 10-20 yards. As we reached the top of the switch backs we ran into a group of mountain goat hunters wearing traditional German attire and exchanged pleasantries at the mouth of the bowl. They must have been VIPs because that was the only time in two years that I ever saw a hunter in the area. A small private cabin exists in the middle of the bowl, and has a traditional "notlager" accessible from the outside as an emergency shelter for hikers and climbers. We stayed the night in the notlager, climbed some the next day, and then headed back to the cars.

Another time we climbed to the Meiler hutte, which is above and to the east of the Oberreintal bowl and we took my battle buddy Ruly and a couple other guys with us. It was more of a hike than a climb, but we gained a lot of elevation quickly and that took its toll on the entire group. About two thirds of the way up we stopped for lunch overlooking the rim of the Oberreintal bowl and were surprised to find an entire company of German soldiers camped out in the bowl. The commander had obviously commandeered the hutte for himself and we were all amazed as a helicopter swooped into the bowl and landed to deliver a senior officer. Even more amazing than that, one of the guys with us accidentally dropped his portable hair dryer out onto the ground while rummaging through his backpack. Jeff and I looked at him in stunned disbelief and asked why he had packed a hairdryer. He just looked back at us and said, "You guys told me we would be staying in a cabin". We all had a good laugh. Continuing up the mountain, which leveled out into a highland meadow for a while, we came across a shepherd with his traditional cloak, staff, two dogs, and a small herd of sheep.

We sluggishly trudged our way up the final draw to the Meiler hutte, which was powered by a wind mill, and we had to actually cross over into Austria to enter the cabin. They had the national border marked with painted lines and a double-sided sign. As we sat there recovering from the 1,600 meters (5,248 feet) of elevation we gained that day a little old German woman crossed over into Austria, walked into the hutte, said, "Ein schnapps bitte!", downed the shot of liquor, dropped her small rucksack, and started talking to everyone like we were all old friends.

The last time I climbed the Zugspitze I led a couple guys from the barracks up the mountain who had been bugging me to take them hiking and climbing all summer long. Casual acquaintances at best, I only felt obligated to take them because one of the guys had introduced me to the Recreational Equipment, Inc. (REI) catalog where I could find more affordable climbing gear than buying it locally. Since he was away on Temporary Duty (TDY) Jeff could not join us. I honestly cannot remember the names of the two guys, but I do remember just being happy we all made it back safely at the end of the weekend. We left the Army base in Augsburg on the Friday evening of Columbus Day weekend and had 3 days to make our ascent and return home. We planned to hike to the Reintalanger Hutte on Saturday, stay the night, climb up past the Knorr Hutte Sunday, make the summit that day and then stay the night at the Knorr Hutte, and finally hike our way back out to the car Monday morning and drive home that afternoon.

When we arrived Friday night the guys insisted on starting our hike immediately instead of waiting until morning, they were quick to point out that we all had headlamps. I eventually relented and we left the olympic stadium and made our way through the Parknachklaum gorge just before dusk and continued hiking until it started snowing and had built up a thin layer on the ground. They only agreed to stop after I explained that our current location was the last comfortable place to camp before the terrain became steep and rocky on both sides of the trail. They pulled out their tent and invited me to join them inside, but I opted for my bivy bag instead so they wouldn't be able to ask me to carry any part of their wet tent later, just because I had slept in it. I laid out my therma-rest sleeping pad, stuffed my goose down sleeping bag into my Gore-Tex bivy bag and went to sleep.

The next morning, Saturday, I woke up thankful for goose down and wool as I brushed the snow off my bivy bag. While heating up water, one of the guys was complaining about the wet snow and how everything was going to be wet and heavy. I just chuckled to myself because I knew I didn't have to carry that tent. After a cold breakfast with some hot tea and coffee we packed up and headed out. We made it to the Reintalanger Hutte early that afternoon and could have easily and safely continued on to the Knorr Hutte, but the guys were wet, cold, and tired from carrying that big wet tent. We sat down for a late lunch and I graciously ordered us all the traditional bergsteigeressen and getrank since they were not members of the Deutscher Aplenverein Sektion Augsburg (Augsburg Chapter of the German Mountain Club) and could not have ordered the discounted meal themselves. The food was hot, filling, and loaded with carbs. As they hung their tent near the stove to dry I stuffed my dry bivy bag into my backpack and spoke to a German who was listening to a weather report on his radio. My bivy bag had dried while we hiked to the hutte because I had draped it over the top of my backpack from side to side knowing that the rising sun at our backs would quickly dry off the Gore-Tex fabric. The German confirmed from the report that the weather would be good and clear the rest of the weekend.

    Sunday morning we awoke to the sound of a hammer dulcimer being played by the cabin master to announce breakfast. I had stayed at the Reintalanger Hutte before and been awaken in the same manner but hadn't realized it was a tradition. We headed up the mountain early, made it past the Knorr Hutte mid-morning, and without stopping headed towards the top of the mountain. We made the summit! I took a group photo of us on the observation deck just below the summit using the timer on my camera and we had some lunch then started back down.

Photo 5: The observation deck of the Zugspitze, that's me on the left.

As we came to the Knorr Hutte the guys indicated they didn't want to stay the night and wanted to hike all the way back to car and drive home that night! I countered that it would be too much for us and wouldn't be safe because of the distance, accelerated pace, and loss of elevation. They said they could make it, so I lied saying I was afraid I couldn't make it. However, we finally agreed to continue back down to the Reintalanger Hutte and stay the night there again. As we approached that hutte the guys informed me they had decided to hike the rest of the way down the valley to the car, and just kept walking. I stopped to rest for a few minutes, took a bite or two of food, and made my decision. Honestly, I really had no choice but to follow them, they were my responsibility and would have probably left me if I stayed the night at the hutte; but, that didn't mean I had to keep up with their accelerated pace. So, I took a deep breath and continued on down the trail at my usual pace. When dusk came I put on my headlamp. I finally arrived at the car about an hour and half after the guys and they were fuming about having to wait for me and threatened they had even considered driving back to the base without me.

I just took another deep breath, placed my backpack in the trunk of the car, and thought about all the critical rules of hiking and mountain climbing they had broken. Prepare for the worst, stay together, set the pace at the slowest person's ability, make a plan and stick to it, do not rush the group; and I added something new to my personal rules. Now, not only would I be extremely selective about who I shoot and hunt with, but I would also be selective of who I take hiking, camping, and mountain climbing.

Chapter 14

Hunting Cabins

Walking down the dirt road between the gate and our cousins' hunting cabin with my father I could barely contain my excitement. The Saturday night before the first day of deer season traditionally brought the men of our family together at our cousins' hunting cabin for fellowship, mountain music, stories, cards, and if you were old enough, beer and some moonshine. As we stepped onto the porch a cousin opened the door and I got my first inside view of a hunting cabin. It was a magical place, dim and hazy from the kerosene lamps, men sitting around in small groups talking or playing cards, old time music drifting through the air, and one guy kicking up sawdust from the cabin floor by flat footin' in the center of the room in front of a wood stove.

  I simply refer to everyone as cousins because that's what they are, there's no need in going into details because whether their second, third, fourth or "removed" cousins doesn't matter. We're all related in one way or another, grew up together, and were raised going to the same churches. There are smaller groups of more closely related cousins within the family, but it didn't matter if you were an Atwell, Grubb, Musser, Gullian, or Cregger you were always welcome at the family reunion and at the Musser's hunting cabin for the Saturday night celebration before the first day of deer season.

  My next exposure to hunting cabins occurred when my Uncle Mike and his friends (including a few cousins) decided to build their own cabin back at the farm in a flat area near the western spring about 150 yards from the tree line of the north ridge. Mike is my dad's baby brother and with only 12 years separating us my Uncle Mike usually let me tag along with him and his friends; everyone called me his "Little Buddy". The Dutton farm loaned us a tractor to dig the post holes, I don't know where the large 20' to 30' posts came from, but the tin sheets of metal we used to make the roof and walls of the hunting cabin came from my grandfather's hay shed. My Paw Paw hadn't used the shed for years, but it's an understatement to say he got upset when he found out that we took his tin without asking. There was a lot of cursing about "them boys" and quite a few "by gods". We insulated the hunting cabin with cardboard, heated it with a large wood stove, and built three stacks of bunks 4 levels high with ladders to get to the topmost bunks.

    Years later we used an old army tent as a hunting cabin, it looked like one of those tents from the movie and TV show M*A*S*H*. After my dad and I stopped working the farm as dairy farmers we converted the milk barn into a hunting cabin and built two bunks into each milking stall. This was a great cabin because it actually had electricity! I took my first deer while camping in that old milk barn. One year we camped on the neighboring farm with some cousins in an old cinderblock building, another year I camped in a simple tent by myself during early archery season, and for a while my Uncle Mike and his friends even bought a camper and used it as a hunting cabin. After coming back from Germany I found that they had even bought an old school bus and converted it into a hunting cabin!

    While all of this crazy cabin building took place in our little circle of friends and cousins, the group of cousins at the Musser cabin up Green Mountain had decided to buy the land next to our farm, turn it into a hunting club, and build a very nice hunting cabin. By this time, in the late 1980s, All Terrain Vehicles (ATVs), 3-wheelers and 4-wheelers were popular and the perceived distance between our farm and their hunting cabin had shrunk significantly. We commonly saw the cousin's headlights as they topped one of the ridges between us heading out to hunt each morning. It looked and sounded like a train rumbling through the mountain. My Uncle Mike used to walk through the woods for hours to get to his favorite hunting spots, but now someone on an ATV could make it there in 30 minutes or less. The hunting club's new hunting lodge, I cannot in good conscience use the word cabin, consisted of a one story cinderblock rambler with a full kitchen and all the modern conveniences. My Uncle Dewey was the only member of the Atwell family to join the club, but not becoming members of the club had no significant impact on my dad and me, at first. Eventually, our annual family reunions shifted from "Aunt Nell's" house to the Rural Retreat Lake when she got older, and then to the hunting lodge after she passed on.

I've now lived in Northern Virginia so long that I had mostly forgotten about the club until my dad told me the club property was for sale in 2011. I would have bought the land and lodge but my money was tied up in other real estate investments, which had been hit hard by the down economy. The family farm now belongs to the pastor of the Lutheran church I grew up in, Saint Paul founded in 1776. I had a chance to buy the farm from my Uncle Dewey before he sold it to the pastor, but I didn't have the financial stability needed at that time because I had already bought 9 acres of my Paw Paws land when he passed away and a small commercial lot in Rural Retreat. It never crossed my mind that I would not be able to hunt back at the farm one day.

At age 26, I built my own hunting cabin on land I bought from Congressman Duncan Hunter, Sr. a Republican and Chairman of the House Armed Services Committee from San Diego, California. The small 2 acre parcel bordered over 4,000 acres of public hunting land and Duncan generously owner financed it for me. My future wife, Amy, helped me build the cabin along with a friend named Gator. We framed the floor on cinderblock pillars, Amy helped me stand up the walls, Gator helped me stand up the trusses, and then we all shingled the 12 in 12 pitch roof. We were on top of a mountain and I didn't want to worry about snow collapsing the roof, plus that steep roof gave us a good sized loft for sleeping and storage. The windows were all old salesman samples from Gator's home improvement business, we heated the cabin the first few years with a large round kerosene heater I got on clearance at Sears, and the siding consisted of cedar planks cut to form a log facade. Standing a few hundred yards from Duncan's hunting lodge my little cabin looked more like a garden shed. Duncan's lodge was made of white oak logs and had a grand fireplace rising up in the middle of the great room. Unfortunately, I never used the cabin much, but my father did come up a couple times, Amy stayed in the cabin a couple times, and I did have a few friends that stayed there too. Eventually, I began to feel like every time I went up to the cabin I had to fix something or do some preventative maintenance and I finally realized that the magic wasn't in cabin itself, but in the family, friends, and traditions that filled it. So, I decided to join a hunting club with some friends who were also hunter education instructors. I sold the land and cabin back to Duncan, who was developing the surrounding land into a subdivision, probably to help fund his Presidential bid in 2008. A couple years later I found another great place to hunt.

    My wife grew up having a "beach house" on the Potomac River, which I assume for her was a lot like me growing up with the farm and hunting cabins. So, when our son was born I decided to find a little place on the Potomac River for all of us. I stumbled across a good deal on some land in Heathsville, Virginia on the Northern Neck. The community had originally been designed as a golf community, but the developer had never gotten around to actually building the golf course. Land ownership in the community included access to the club house, a narrow stretch of beach, swimming pool, tennis courts, basketball court, driving range, fishing pier, boat ramp, boat slips, campground, and hunting area. Yes, I said campground and hunting area! Amy loves the place, which is just down and across the Potomac River from her old beach house in St. Mary's County on the Maryland side. We will eventually build a house on our lot, but for now we are content to stay in a camper in the campground, use the shared boat ramp and boat slips for crabbing with our sailboat, and going deer hunting with the family in the hunting area. Next Year it will be me, my son Wyatt, nephew Kobe, and maybe even my brother-in-law David or sister Annie camping out and hunting deer together. If we can swing it I would love to eventually have all my nieces and nephews join us!

Chapter 15

Which is more important, the shooter or the rifle?

    The instructor, a Marine Corps Sniper, walked over to the shooter next to me to check the guy's rifle and I couldn't help but hope that guy's shots were the ones key holing at 1,000 yards instead of mine. The range safety officer in the target pits had radioed back to the firing line that shooter #4 needed to stop shooting because his bullets were tumbling inaccurately into the target, key holing, and causing a potentially unsafe situation for the relay of shooters currently working the pits. The instructor came to me first even though I was shooter #5 because my rifle had caused some concern at the beginning of the class the day before. I had to defend the capabilities of my custom built rifle based on a Mauser Action with a .308 WIN chamber, and a 26" bull barrel by strongly stating it could shoot just as good as any of the modern Savage, Remington, and FN rifles in the class. On the firing line that day, the instructor finally moved on, but only after I pointed out that I was not shooter #4, my barrel was at least 6 inches longer that shooter #4's, I was using commercially manufactured match grade Federal .308 WIN Match King ammunition with a 172 grain boat tailed bullet, and that Shooter #4 was using hand loaded ammunition that had never been tested at 1,000 yards. After speaking extensively with Shooter #4 the instructor spoke into his radio, gave me the "GO" sign, and when Shooter #4 started packing up his gear I knew I could start shooting again.

That training experience at the Quantico Shooting Club as part of a 1,000 yard marksmanship class tops my list of the best days ever spent learning to shoot. I wasn't the best shooter in the class, but I wasn't the worst either which says a lot considering the cost of my rifle and optics totaled out at about $800 and everyone else shot rifles and optics that weekend costing over $2,500. The class also reminded me of something my Paw Paw once said, "It doesn't take a fancy rifle to be a good shooter, you just have to have a good one, and shoot it a lot." He was talking about my Uncle Mike at the time, who has a habit of always buying the latest and greatest gun, bow, and/or scope. I had been telling Paw Paw about Mike's latest shooting miracle. He had shot a very nice 8 point buck over half way up the south ridge of the farm from a corner fence post near the north ridge, easily a 300+ yard shot, almost all the way across the farm. Paw Paw was unimpressed and simply stated, "By god, if he would just stick to one rifle imagine how good he would be (at shooting)!" and took a drink of homemade wine.

The 1,000 Yard class also proved my father's point that you have to "Aim Small" to "Miss Small"; meaning you have to concentrate acutely on all aspects of shooting and choose a very small aiming point to be successful. We spent two days learning and documenting the dope for our rifles in our log books; shooting at 100 yards, 200 yards, 400 yards, 600 yards, 800 yards, and then finally at 1000 yards. My rifle case doubled as a shooting mat because we shot from the prone position and my backpack full of extra clothes, water, lunch, and ammo acted as a gun rest. The instructor did not recommend bi-pods because they were actually very hard to use effectively. I still keep the target we shot at 800 and 1000 yards at work in my desk, just in case one of the guys at work wants to start bragging about their shooting ability. A few of my shots hit the 8" diamond bullseye at both 800 and 1000 yards, but all of my shots were on the paper and most would have hit a real life size target.

Chapter 16

Army Marksmanship

Sitting in the First Sergeant's office after returning from emergency leave I asked him again, "Ain't there anything you can do? I really don't want to start basic training all over again." Top just shook his head and told me again how sorry he was my mother had passed away and how anyone missing two weeks of training had to be recycled. I asked him what type of training I missed and he told me Basic Rifle Marksmanship had started the day after I left and the entire company qualifies in two days then asked me, "Have you every shot a rifle before?" Sensing an opportunity, I leaned in towards the First Sergeant and boldly announced, "I've been shooting my whole life and I know I can qualify with the rest of the company!" Top sat back is his chair, thinking for a moment, and told me he needed to talk to the company commander.

    While I waited I mentally made a list of talking points and reminded myself that I had negotiated my way into graduating high school six months early the previous year, so I could definitely talk my way out of this situation too. I figured I would tell the Commanding Officer (CO) that I had already been issued my individual weapon and attended the rifle familiarization and safety class before going on emergency leave, plus I'd been shooting and hunting since I was three years old. None of this was necessary. Top came back with the CO and she asked me if I really thought I could qualify in two days and I said, "Yes ma'am, no problem." She nodded and informed me I would be joining another company for training the next day and if I successfully qualified with our company the day after that I could continue basic training with my current platoon and would not be recycled.

Now keep in mind I had never touched an M-16 rifle until a few days before my mom died, two weeks earlier, and had never actually shot one. The only Army training I had received at that point included the basic disassembly, reassembly, function check, loading, and unloading of a M-16. The next morning Top had me ride in a truck out to the ranges and assigned a Drill Sergeant from another company to work with me all day long. I shot for hours that day and initially had some trouble with the rear peep site, which I had never used before. The front site was also confusing because of the wings on each side of the front site post that protected it. However, the Drill Sergeant continued to work with me and we zeroed my rifle at 25 meters then we moved on to another range so I could shoot at some targets further away.

I rejoined my company on qualification day, but didn't know quite what to expect and looking back I feel a little like Forrest Gump. I just got in line with everyone else in my platoon, held my rifle, waited for my turn to shoot, and said, "Yes Drill Ser - geant!" a lot. When everyone else moved forward I moved forward. If everyone else had jumped off a cliff with their rifles that day I would have probably done the same thing.

The qualification firing point consisted of a fox hole dug into an elevated mound of dirt, so none of us could really see what was going on until we were the next person in line to shoot. When I became the next shooter I watched the soldier in front of me very closely. As he started shooting I noticed he had trouble with magazine reloads because he had placed his extra magazines on the right side of the gun, but had to reload with his left hand. I decided I would place my magazines on the left side of the gun so I could reload faster. Then I saw the targets!

Like I said, I had no idea what to expect. I had not received the training and briefings that everyone else had, so when the targets starting popping up for the shooter in front of me I had to watch him and figure it all out for myself. The targets were life size silhouettes of a man's upper body. The closer ones popping up at

50 and 100 meters were silhouettes from the shoulders up and the ones from 150 meters to 300 meters were from the waste up. The targets would pop up and remain visible for a few seconds and then fall back down. I finally started to relax a little when I realized that the qualification was going to be a lot like groundhog hunting back home. I used to walk through hay fields in the summer time watching for woodchucks to stand up on their hind legs to look around, and only had a few seconds to shoot at them before they dropped back down out of sight.

To qualify we were given 40 targets, 40 rounds of ammunition (5 per magazine), and had to hit 23 targets to qualify and earn our Marksmanship badge. Higher level badges were awarded for more targets; 30+ received a Sharp Shooter badge and 36+ received an Expert badge. In order to improve my chances of qualifying I decided that if I missed any of the closer targets I would shoot at them again and not shoot at one of the 300 meter targets. There are not a lot of 300+ yard shots in the Blue Ridge Mountains of Virginia, so I did not want to waste ammo on targets I would most likely miss.

My turn! I ran up the berm, jumped in the fox hole, arranged my magazines as planned, and got into a good firing position. The foxhole provided a surprisingly stable shooting platform and the course of fire went by so fast it was all just a blur. I do remember hitting at least one 300 meter target, I even hollered, "Yeah!" when I hit it. I ended up qualifying as a Sharp Shooter, not Expert, but not Marksman either. Pretty good considering I missed two weeks of training.

Another guy from my home town, Tim, ended up in the same basic training platoon with me and had also shot really well during qualification. When the Company Commander and First Sergeant came around to officially inform me I could continue basic training with my platoon they also remarked on the incredible marksmanship ability of Tim and Me. They jokingly asked if there were any more boys back home like us and I simply responded, "Yes Ma'am, lot's of them!"

While stationed in Germany I had an opportunity to train with the German Army and try to earn their Marksmanship badge, the "Schützenschnur". To qualify for the Schützenschnur you have to shoot their service pistol, rifle, and machine gun. This usually required two joint training exercises and only two of these exercises were held each year. Late in the summer of 1994 I participated in one of the joint exercises and easily qualified with their pistol and rifle, but we didn't have time to shoot the machine gun. Unfortunately, I transferred back to the states before we held another joint exercise, so I never completed the qualification course of fire for the Schützenschnur. Although I didn't earn a badge I did get to see my first fully baffled rifle range; the 1,000 meter range with firing points and overhead baffles to stop errant bullets every 100 meters made quite a spectacular sight.

After returning to the states and being stationed at Fort Myers, near Arlington National Cemetery, I had to requalify with the M-16 rifle. Since my new unit mostly worked in the Pentagon or high rise office buildings in the Washington, DC area no proper range existed for qualification and we had to use a small 25 meter indoor range at Fort Belvoir and shoot the alternate "C" course. This alternate course consisted of a special paper target with 10 different silhouettes on it scaled to represent the targets at various distances from 50 meters to 300 meters. Each silhouette has a 4 centimeter (CM) circle drawn in the middle of it, probably because the standard for zeroing a M-16 is 5 out of 6 shots in a 4 CM circle. The M-16s used on the alternate course of fire have .22 long rifle adapter kits installed and the objective is to place 4 shots in each black silhouette during an allotted amount of time. Shots are fired from both the prone supported and unsupported positions, 2 shots per target in each position.

I took my time and did well, but a soldier next to me had some trouble and complained half way through the course of fire that he could not hit the smaller targets and probably wouldn't qualify. I told him to relax, take his time shooting, and that all the targets were actually the same size. He looked at me like I was crazy, so I explained to him the center of each silhouette had a 4 CM circle in it, the same circle he had hit 5 out of 6 times to zero his rifle, and that he should be aiming at that circle in the center of the silhouettes and not the silhouettes themselves. He thanked me and said he would try it. After completing the course of fire we both felt confident as we walked down range to check our targets.

The soldier next to me qualified, but barely squeaked by and kept thanking me profusely. The range sergeant counted up my hits and came up with 39 out of 40, which impressed my new friend but left me wanting a little more. I asked the sergeant to count again and he still came up with 39, so I asked to see the target and was told I couldn't touch the target until after the score had been officially recorded. He also told me I could take any concerns up with the Non-Commissioned Officer In Charge (NCOIC) of the range, which I later found out happened to be a Platoon Sergeant (Sergeant First Class) with an attitude.

I reviewed my target and found my 40th shot, which had actually cut through another bullet hole. I pointed it out to the NCOIC who glanced at it and said, "I don't think so." So, I flipped the target over and pointed out that the two concentric bullet holes were more obvious from the back. He responded, "You could have done that with a pencil." Starting to get aggravated I mentioned that a pencil would not have left a ring of carbon around the bullet hole and he just shook his head. Finally, I couldn't take it anymore and coldly said in a firm voice, "Sergeant, so you are telling me that I'm such a great shot that not only did I hit 39 out of 40 targets, but also kept all of my shots in the 4 CM circle, however, I just happened to shoot one shot so bad that it completely missed the entire sheet of paper?" The sergeant turned towards me with fire in his eyes and responded, "That's right Specialist, now get off my range!" Luckily, my new buddy and a couple other friends grabbed me by the arms and pulled me out the front door of the range. Otherwise, I probably would have ended up in a lot of trouble that day and hauled away by the MPs (Military Police). Sometimes, being right just isn't worth the cost, especially when you are dealing with someone on a power trip.

Chapter 17

Oh Crappie!

Half listening to my father's instructions on how to fish with a rubber worm I stared across the water of a small farm pond and could not wait to make the first cast. I loved to go fishing with my dad, especially in new ponds and creeks. He finally stopped talking and we started fishing. He had shown me how to hook the worm through the middle so that the two ends hung evenly on both sides of the hook; one end had a curled flat tail on it that would spin as the worm moved through the water. We used black worms with red tails that day, but my father also liked to use purple worms with pink tails.

I cast my line out and reeled it in, over and over again, but got no bites. Dad would occasionally reel in a fish and holler over some more instructions, "Don't reel it in so fast; reel for a few seconds then stop for a second or two; when you cast let the worm sink to the bottom before you start reeling; sometimes they hit on the way down." We slowly walked around the pond by moving to the right a couple steps every 2-3 casts and dad gradually worked himself further around the pond until he was directly across from me about 20 yards away. Casting towards the center of the pond we both fished the same spot, about 10 yards away from each of us in the center of the pond.

Remembering what my father had told me, I finally started to control my impulse to start reeling and allowed the worm to sink to the bottom after hitting the water. Then, it suddenly happened, my worm didn't sink to the bottom; I got a strong hit! Taken completely by surprise I barely had the wits to set the hook before I started reeling. I guess my dad could tell I had a big one, because he was standing by my side by the time I got the fish to the edge of the pond. We both got excited; it was the biggest Crappie either of us had ever seen, over a foot long, and to this day the biggest Crappie I have ever caught.

Chapter 18

My First Spring Gobbler

On the crisp spring morning that I took my first gobbler a Tom turkey had responded to both my crow calls and owl calls from the western side of the north ridge. My dad had just dropped me off at the milk barn and before walking up the long incline to the north ridge I wanted to know if there were any gobblers nearby, and if so, where they were. Instead of making a bee line towards the turkey I decided to take the long way around so I could setup a better hunting position. I walked straight up the eastern side of the north ridge to the big pine tree, took a left, and walked westward on the top of the ridge. Once I got close to the northwest corner of the farm I dropped down off the ridgeline onto the southern slope, positioned myself about half way down the ridge with my back against a tree, and started calling.

The gobbler responded well to my calls and slowly made his way towards me. After what seemed an eternity he came into sight west of me and down the ridge a little with his tail feathers all spread out like a peacock. I groaned to myself because it's harder to call a gobbler up hill and the more you try the warier they get. However, I coaxed him into about 50 yards, but then he started to strut back and forth. I groaned again because the limit for my shotgun with an extra full turkey choke was about 50 yards and once a gobbler starts strutting they rarely come any closer. So, I decided to take the shot, BOOM!

The gobbler started running so I took a second shot and this time he started flopping. I jumped up, ran over to the turkey, and shot him one last time in the head to put him out of his misery. I couldn't believe it; I got my first spring gobbler! I tagged him and carried him down to the milk barn, this time I took the shortest route possible. My dad picked me up later that morning and he drove me to my uncle's gas station at Staley Crossroads to check in the turkey. My Uncle Mike had a completely different reaction to the turkey.

When we arrived at his store my Uncle Mike was initially very excited, until he saw the bird. Then he started asking questions about where I shot it and started messing around with the wings, lifting them up, and looking under them. I told him the whole story and then he just started mumbling, "I'm sorry Adam, I'm so sorry". My family calls me Adam, my middle name. I looked at him in puzzlement and Uncle Mike humbly explained that one of our cousins was supposed to have gotten that gobbler. It turns out he and his friends had bought a turkey at a local farm and chosen it because it had no white feathers and looked like a wild turkey. Then, they pinned a note under its wing and released it back at the farm to play a trick on one of our cousins, the same cousin who had recently accidentally shot his own truck three times. I'll tell you more about that truck incident later, but for now, suffice it to say I saved him from even more embarrassment that day. The note, which must have fallen off because we never found it, had read, "Now look what you've did, you've done gone and shot my tame turkey!" Ever the optimist, I told my Uncle Mike that I didn't care because I had called the gobbler in just the way he had taught me and the turkey had responded just like I would have expected a wild turkey to respond. We've laughed about that turkey for years, but spring turkey hunting never really stuck with me and I rarely do it anymore. I don't know why, but I would rather just go fishing.

Chapter 19

Catfishing

No cats were harmed in the writing of this chapter; and although you can entertain a cat for long periods of time using a fishing pole and something bright and colorful tied to the end of the line, this is not that type of story. Catfishing or "Catfishin'" as it usually sounds is a southern word, a verb, for specifically going after catfish and it usually occurs at night time. The most common type of catfishing includes going out with a few buddies to a secluded spot on a lake, pond, or river; sitting around in lantern light or campfire light until late hours of the night; reeling in the catfish; and if you're a drinker having a few beers. If you have a really good fishing hole you have very little time to drink beer because you're always reeling in the cats!

Most people use raw chicken livers as catfish bait because they are inexpensive and the blood attracts the catfish. Some people use shrimp, which my father and I never really understood. Shrimp is expensive and I would rather eat shrimp than catfish! However, on a warm spring day my father accidentally discovered why shrimp is such good catfish bait, but I'll tell you more about that a little later. The trick to fishing with chicken livers is to use a large hook and have a gentle sloping cast that throws the bait a long distance without throwing it off the hook. The catfish swim along the bottom of the water scavenging for food and will pick up the chicken liver and usually swim out towards deeper water with it. The art of catfishing comes down to knowing when to actually set the hook. If you wait too long the catfish will swallow the chicken liver and hook resulting in gut hooking and if you jerk too soon you rip the chicken liver in half losing both the catfish and the bait because the catfish hadn't gotten the hook in its mouth yet.

    My wife, Amy, and I used to go night catfishing at Burke Lake in Fairfax, Virginia and found a great spot near their boat ramp where you could literally catch 2-3 pound catfish all night long, and occasionally catch a much bigger one. We would sit there for hours in camping chairs just reeling them in; they hit so fast and so hard we had trouble keeping up with them when using two fishing poles. One time we accidentally left the lantern at home, and I really showed my redneck side. I had placed the lantern by the front door so we could grab it on the way out; I thought I had asked Amy to grab it, but may not have done so. Half way to the lake I suddenly thought about the lantern and asked Amy if she grabbed it, she responded, "No". I threw an Atwell temper tantrum, made a fool of myself, and drove over to Wal-Mart to buy a new lantern because the store was closer than driving home. What an idiot I was, it's hard to believe that I got that upset over a forgotten lantern. I am very lucky she loves me and still married me after that fiasco.

    My father ran out of bait once while fishing on the dam of Rural Retreat Lake and decided to scavenge for some. The waterline at the dam, like most manmade lakes, is rocky to prevent erosion and after flipping over a few rocks my dad scooped up a crawdad and decided to fish with it. Dad hooked it through the tail with the hook coming out of the top, placed a bobber about 4 feet up from the hook, and then cast the crawdad about 10 feet out. After a few minutes the bobber disappeared and dad reeled in a nice catfish. I started doing the same and we caught a lot of fish that spring, and saved a lot of money on bait. Over time we also caught bass and muskies at the dam using crawdads. The secret is to setup your line and cast it out just far enough that the crawdad is bouncing around on top of the rocks, but also cannot get enough grip to actually crawl under a rock. Unlike night catsfishing there is no art to setting the hook, when your bobber disappears you just jerk the pole; and let me tell you that bobber vanishes suddenly and goes completely out of sight. Over the years we found late spring and early summer to be the best time of year and have always done this type of catfishing during the day.

Now you know why catfish will hit on shrimp, they're scavengers and they really like crawdads, shrimp's country cousin. Like I said my dad and I like shrimp too, so one day we decided to try some crawdads. We waited until night time walked up to the dam of the lake with a flashlight, net, and 5 gallon bucket, and filled it up within an hour. At night time the crawdads just lay on top of the rocks! We boiled up that mess of crawdads, melted some butter, and ate like kings that night.

Chapter 20

My Best Friend

No safari would be complete without a love story. This one may not be of epic proportions, but it does start with a tragedy and ultimately ends with a passionate couple that lives happily ever after. I met my best friend at a saloon in northern Virginia where music played until the early morning hours, drinks flowed like water, and the Texas swing, two step, and waltz were all danced to the music I played. Her friends had tried to introduce us for weeks, but she rarely came out to the club because of work and school. Amelia, Amy to her friends, already had an associate's degree in nursing and a license as a Registered Nurse, but still worked as a floor secretary at a local hospital while completing her bachelor's degree. However, none of this really mattered to me at the time because my marriage of less than a year had recently unraveled leaving me with no interest in starting any new relationships.

I now believe everyone in the military should be entitled to one bad marriage and that everyone else should give them a mulligan on it. Young Soldiers, Sailors, Airmen, and Marines tend to live life on the edge, make impulsive decisions, take quick action, and usually do not have enough life experience to do any of these things very well. After two and a half years in the Army, most of it overseas, I came back to the states and married a nice young lady I met during my senior year of high school. Looking back, I now see we were doomed from the start. I wanted to be a renaissance man and experience everything life had to offer while she just wanted to get away from her family; even though they treated her like a princess. After just a few months of marriage my first wife announced she wanted to go back home and stay with her mom and dad for a while. Realizing that things had not worked out well since she decided to become a housewife instead of a student or professional I gave her an ultimatum; stay and we would work things out or go and never come back. She chose the latter and we divorced within a year, honestly, we were just too young for marriage. Luckily, no children blessed our union and it lasted less than a year so our small calamity paled in comparison to most divorces which liken to a greek tragedy or the fifth act of a shakespearean play when everyone dies or become destitute. However, I do consider my first marriage and resulting divorce akin to the third act of a shakespearean tragedy, where a death, in this case the death of my first marriage, is necessary to setup the rest of the story. In an ironic twist of fate my first wife's name was also Amy, but that is the only similarity between the two of them.

    The first time I met my best friend and soul mate I remember thinking to myself, "Now that's the type of woman I should go out with"; but keep in mind that I seriously had no interest in dating anyone at the time. We exchanged pleasantries and shook hands as Amelia's (Amy's) girlfriends giggled. I still remember how beautiful she looked with her sandy blonde hair hanging down over her shoulders, head tilted at a slight angle, and gleaming white smile. I also remember thinking that I really liked her teeth. Amy had persistent friends and we ended up spending New Year's Eve together with her friends at the saloon, even though I had to work. Amy also started coming out to the club more often. In between setting up songs I would sneak out on the dance floor with her, one of her friends, or some other lady to dance a fast Texas swing or two step; but Amy doesn't dance much so we eventually ended up talking a lot and I began dancing less and less each night. Amy and I went to a few concerts with her friends and would somehow always end up sitting beside each other.

    One night, after a concert, I took Amy home and we spent hours sitting in her living room looking at photo albums and scrap books while we talked about our time in high school drama class and our trips to Europe. We went horseback riding once, which I later found out scared Amy to death, but she went anyway. We went to see "Much Ado About Nothing" and "Romeo & Juliet" at the Shakespeare Theater in Washington, DC. We went to her family's beach house in Saint Mary's County, Maryland and fished with her dad on the lower Potomac. We even went night catfishing at Burke Lake in Fairfax and camping in Luray, Virginia; both of which tended to showcase my redneck side. However, she always said yes whenever I asked her out. We even drove half way across the country to Fort Leavenworth, Kansas in my pickup truck to see some Army friends of mine. Along the way we camped in Cherokee, North Carolina and Nashville, Tennessee. We fished for Trout on the Cherokee reservation and explored the Opryland hotel in Nashville.

Photo 6: My best friend and wife, Amy.

David Adam Atwell

  The first time I told Amy I loved her it just spontaneously came out of me with no premeditation or control. She stood in the doorway of my apartment's bathroom primping for a concert, turned towards me, tilted her head sideways, asked "How do I look?", and then smiled. My heart melted as I softly responded, "I love you", without realizing I had said the words out loud. Love at first sight used to sound like hyperbole to me, but I now earnestly believe that I fell in love with Amy the first time I saw her at the saloon. When I recall our first moment together it is as if a sea of people parted and Amy appeared in front of me like an angel from heaven.

  We married in the spring of 1999 at the main street gazebo in Front Royal, Virginia and had our reception at the Stadt Kaffe, a German restaurant across the street. Just before the wedding, and unknown to me, my father asked Amy if she really wanted to go through with it and she still said yes. We delayed our honeymoon for a year because we had paid for the wedding and reception ourselves without going into debt; and having just received her bachelor's degree and gaining some nursing work experience Amy was about to start her career as an operating room nurse. A year later we celebrated our first anniversary in fabulous Las Vegas, Nevada, saw the Grand Canyon from the air and toured Hoover Dam. Our son, Wyatt, was born in May 2008, shortly after Amy completed her master's degree. All of our birthdays are in early May, so our home is full of bullish and steadfast love, devotion, and loyalty for each other and the people and ideas closest to our hearts. My love of Amy makes me want to be a better man and I can no longer imagine a life without her and Wyatt by my side. Amy is truly my best friend.

* * * * *

The Summer Sun

The first time I told you I loved you,
It spontaneously came out of me,
With no premeditation or control.

You stood in the doorway of my home,
With your head tilted slightly to the side,
And melted my heart with your radiance.

Your smile lit a fire within me akin to the summer sun
And I softly proclaimed my love for you,
Without realizing I had spoken the words aloud.

Chapter 21

Hunting the Great American Buffalo

American Bison, or Buffalo as they are commonly called, made a resurgence in late 20th century after almost being hunted to extinction by greedy commercial hunters out west in the late 1800s and hungry colonists back east in the 18th and 17th centuries. The smaller Woods Buffalo used to roam freely throughout Virginia, and small herds were hunted in the Shenandoah Valley by early settlers. However, Virginia's buffalo all disappeared by the end of the 1700s because they were easy to harvest and provided colonists with easy access to food. There were a lot of new immigrants settling in Virginia at the time, including the Atwells in the early 1600s, and they all had to eat.

Conservationists and sportsmen around the country finally realized that the remaining bison herds needed protection and formed conservationist clubs, national forests and parks, farms, and ranches to help in their preservation. When the lean meat craze took hold of the country in the 1990s free range buffalo meat became an appealing alternative to farm raised beef and the bison farmers and ranchers suddenly had a cash crop, well a cash herd. By the dawn of the 21st century restaurants and grocery stores started offering buffalo steaks and buffalo burgers, some restaurants even dedicated their entire menu to buffalo. The new publicity surrounding buffalo meat also sparked renewed interest in buffalo hunting in the hearts of some Americans. Movies romanticizing the old west lifestyle and buffalo hunting, such as

Dances with Wolves, Wyatt Earp, and Legends of the Fall probably helped spur hunters and ranchers into action.

    A good farmer and rancher knows they have to routinely cull their herd to keep it healthy, productive, and growing. The unwanted or unneeded animals are usually sold at market, but bison ranchers eventually realized that some hunters are willing to pay more than the market price for an opportunity to hunt buffalo. My personal experience in this area involves a rancher in Pingree, North Dakota; his place is called "The Bison Ranch at Couteau Ridge". Oren's ranch is about 4,000 acres and he has about 300 bison.

    When invited by my friends at the NORVA Rod & Gun Club to join them on a buffalo hunt I initially struggled with the ethics of hunting such a rare and beautiful animal. However, as a conservationist I ultimately believe in the preservation and sustainable use of natural resources, and that includes wildlife like the American Bison; which after all had been saved from extinction by the very ranchers and farmers who now offer buffalo hunts. I finally rationalized that by going to a well-respected and well managed ranch and paying the rancher more money than he would receive at the market for the same buffalo that I would actually be helping preserve at least one buffalo herd. Plus, it would really be cool! How many Americans actually get to go hunting for buffalo these days?

    I packed up all my cold weather winter gear and two .308 rifles and left Manassas, Virginia with a friend named Mike in the early morning of January 9, 2007. We ran into snow in the Allegheny Mountains heading towards Pittsburgh, Pennsylvania and actually made it to Chicago, Illinois in about 10 hours. It took just over 2 days driving to get all the way to Pingree, North Dakota which is about an hour slightly northwest of Fargo. I enjoyed seeing the monolithic rock outcroppings in Wisconsin that are similar to the sandstone hoodoos out west, but consisting of harder rock. Crossing the Mississippi River in Minneapolis, Minnesota surprised me because the river was so narrow that far north. We stopped in Fargo, North Dakota to purchase our hunting licenses and since my wife loves the movie Fargo I also had to buy her a shot glass for her collection.

Oren met us at the "hunting cabin" he provides for his guests, it's really a Sears kit house built in 1912. His father purchased the house from a neighbor and used a team of 8 horses to drag it onto their family ranch where it sits today. We went out to dinner at the only local tavern, called the "281 Stop", which is actually a cooperative restaurant owned and managed by the people in the community. The rest of the NORVA group did not arrive until the following day.

The next morning Oren fixed us a hearty breakfast, which was included in the cost of the hunt, and then took Mike and I out for our buffalo hunt. We drove his old white pickup truck out into the fields looking for the herd because he said the bison were used to the white truck and it would not startle them. We eventually found the herd and Oren started identifying which bison were available to us. He knew them all and honestly said we could harvest any bison we wanted, but would have to pay the fair market value of the animal. He then informed us that a previous hunter had once "accidentally" shot one of his prize winning breeding bulls and had to pay thousands of dollars for the animal. Mike and I were hunting for meat and since all buffalo, male and female, have horns we weren't worried about taking big trophies. Oren started pointing out the buffalo heifers he planned to take to market at the end of the hunting season and reminded us that those animals were the best value.

Mike graciously offered to let me take the first shot, so after picking out a couple bison I got out of the truck and setup a good shooting position in front of the truck. Mike took up a position behind the truck. We patiently waited for an opportunity to take our shots, but none presented themselves. The bison were just too close to each other; to take an ethical and safe shot you have to wait for the buffalo you want to move away from the herd. You cannot shoot into the herd because you would wound multiple animals, potentially cause a stampede, and also have to pay for every wounded animal. Oren recommended we reposition ourselves to get a better view of the herd, so Mike and I climbed back into the truck. Oren drove around to the west side of the herd to give us a better vantage.

    While identifying which buffalo we wanted from our new location we saw another truck suddenly appear in the field and that spooked the herd. The bison all stopped grazing and started deliberately walking towards a small gap in the surrounding hills. The new truck contained the rest of the NORVA hunting party, who had just arrived and decided to drive out to look at the buffalo. Realizing that the spooked herd would soon be out of sight and out of range, Oren told us that if we wanted to take a shot we better do it now. I jumped out of the truck again, moved forward, identified my buffalo, waited for a clean shot, and took it. The buffalo slowed down, but did not stop. Oren coaxed me to shoot again, so I worked the bolt on my modified .308 Mauser Action mountain rifle, lined up the express sites, and fired again. Another hit, this time the buffalo stopped walking. Adrenaline pumping, I didn't wait for Oren this time and reloaded and shot again. This time the buffalo dropped to the ground and stopped moving altogether. The other bison around mine also stopped and stood with their fallen comrade for a minute or two, as if to pay their final respects, and then moved on. Later on, Oren informed me I probably didn't need that last shot after the buffalo stopped, because it usually takes a couple seconds for them to actually fall down. I responded that after hearing his story about once chasing a wounded, and adrenaline driven, buffalo for miles I wanted to make sure my buffalo did not get away, and of course did not suffer.

    Meanwhile, Mike had gotten setup and started taking his shots. I painfully watched as a couple clouds of dust puffed up when he missed. To be honest I think I hampered his efforts a little by accidentally getting in his way and bumping into him. As the last of the herd disappeared over the hills we walked up to my buffalo. I paced it off at about 106 yards, which was a good shot. Most people don't understand that when hunting dangerous game you want to be close because that increases your chances of successfully taking the animal with one shot, or in my case a few shots. Dangerous game such as bear, buffalo, and lions are rarely taken at long distances with a scoped rifle, and at 106 yards I had pushed the limit. We drove back to the cabin, met up with the rest of the NORVA group, and used a John Deere tractor to retrieve my buffalo. Mike went out again that afternoon and took his buffalo. Mike and Oren had to go find the herd using the tractor that afternoon because, after the morning's events, the truck would have made the herd skittish. The butcher who processed my buffalo later told us that two of my bullets had actually hit the buffalo's heart and that the first shot had been about a foot behind the heart.

The next day the rest of the NORVA group went on their buffalo hunts while I updated my field journal. I also went coyote hunting that afternoon. I really had no interest in shooting a coyote, but I liked the idea of being alone outside in the snow and sub-zero temperatures doing nothing except relaxing and thinking. I grabbed my sporterized long distance .308 Mauser bolt action rifle, with a scope, strapped its case on my back and walked a little over a mile from the cabin to a double stack of round hay bales. I climbed up on top the bales and made a nice sniper's nest between two of them.

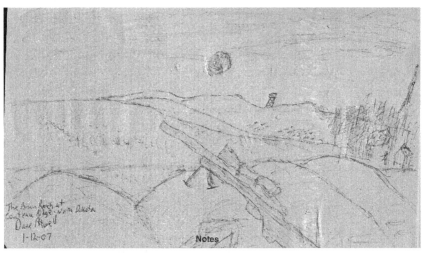

Photo 7: A sketch of The Bison Ranch at Couteau Ridge

I stood, sat, and laid there comfortably for hours sheltered from the wind and dressed in my wool long johns, hunting parka and bibs, and a goose down vest. It was 14 degrees below zero. I never saw any coyotes, but I did draw a small sketch of my view from the hay bales which I have included above. I stayed there until dark and only left when I saw a truck's headlights leave the cabin and head towards me. About 5 minutes later Oren stopped and offered me a ride back to the cabin. I thanked him and asked if he minded me walking the rest of the way. He just nodded and turned the truck around. The North Dakota sky is a beautiful sight to behold on a clear night.

    I brought home 448 pounds of meat from that hunt and used half of the tanned buffalo hide to make a buffalo fur vest, hat, and possibles bag for myself and an arrow quiver for my dad to use with his recurve bow. I am planning to loan the other half of the buffalo hide to the Wolf Creek Indian Village to use in their museum displays; it's a very big hide. While I did pay a tanner to work up the hide for me I personally worked the buffalo horns myself. After patiently and carefully taking a couple weeks to remove them from the skull I hand worked them into powder horns and polished them to a fine sheen using ashes from my fireplace. I kept one of the horns for myself and gave the other to a friend named Jimmy who uses it in Revolutionary War reenactments. I'm sure he's proud as a peacock whenever people ask him why he has a black powder horn and he gets to tell them how buffalo powder horns would have been common in colonial Virginia during the revolutionary war because there were still buffalo in Virginia at that time.

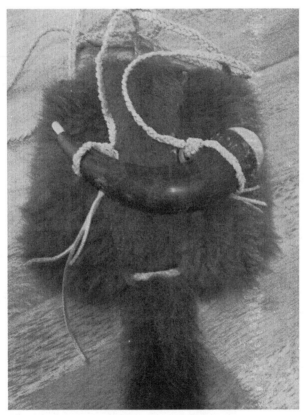

Photo 8: The possibles bag and powder horn made from my buffalo.

Chapter 22

Staying Warm in a Hunting Blind

    I took my nephew Kobe on his first hunting trip at age 6. We started out squirrel hunting and then worked our way up to deer hunting. Already proficient with a BB gun, I decided to upgrade Kobe to a single shot hinge action .410 shotgun. The gun really belonged to my son, but since Wyatt wouldn't be born until May I didn't think he would mind. The shotgun kicked a little harder than Kobe liked, but he could hit targets with it. Later that year I gave Kobe the same model gun for Christmas, a Rossi "Matched Pair". A hinge action gun with two removable barrels, one in .410 shotgun and the other in .22 long rifle. Until he gets older Kobe has to hunt with his gun unloaded and I only give him a shell when it's actually time to shoot. Sometimes he will miss out on game this way, but it's much safer and teaches him the patience necessary to wait and take only the good shoots that harvest animals cleanly without a lot of suffering.
    The first morning, we went squirrel hunting on the ridge above the hunting cabin and only got a shot at one squirrel. The squirrel was a pesky fellow that kept coming out of hiding whenever we walked past but would hide as soon as we stopped or turned his way. We had to split up and walk in different directions to confuse and trick him, but it eventually worked and we got our shot. The squirrel fell to the ground but started to scurry away

when we got close, so David, Kobe's dad, stepped on its tail and I quickly reached down and slit its throat with my pocket knife to end its suffering. I started showing Kobe how to field dress the squirrel and he turned white as a ghost and almost passed out. However, we still had scrambled eggs and squirrel for breakfast when we got back to the cabin!

    The next morning we went deer hunting in a blind I had setup. Like most kids Kobe got bored real quick and we did a lot of muffled talking to keep him interested in hunting. It takes a lot of patience to hunt from a tree stand or hunting blind. After a while Kobe also started to get cold, but I was ready for him and pulled out a blaze orange goose down vest from my backpack. I know from personal experience how the cold air can drain all your energy and concentration while just sitting around waiting for deer. I grew up without a lot of money for fancy hunting clothes, but my saving grace as a young hunter had been my dad's hand me down "Big Red" quilted hunting coat my mother had handmade. Wearing Big Red was like being wrapped up in a stack of winter quilts.

    I had Kobe stand up and zipped him into the goose down vest, which covered him from shoulders to ankles because it was so big. I guess it really warmed Kobe up, because when I looked over at him a few moments later his eyes were closed and his head rested against a log. He had fallen asleep! He looked like the great pumpkin from a Charlie Brown cartoon huddled in the corner of the hunting blind in that big poofy orange vest.

* * * * *

A color version of the following photo is available on the Appalachian Safari website and Facebook page.

http://www.appalachiansafari.com/

http://www.facebook.com/myappalachiansafari

Photo 9: Staying warm in a hunting blind.

Chapter 23

Trekkin' and Pickin' with the Old Grey Owl

     I spent a few summers in my youth hiking with an older gentleman from my church named Randal, he was also known as the "Old Grey Owl". The first time I went hiking with him it was actually on a Llama Trek with a youth group from church and we all had a lot of fun. I remember thinking llamas were cool because they all stopped together on the trail to use the bathroom at the same time and they spit on you when they were aggravated. At the end of the llama trek Randal gave each of us a sierra cup that he had engraved for us himself. I still have mine and it has travelled all over the world with me. His sierra cup had made quite an impression on all of us kids during the trip; a sierra cup is really more like a bowl than a cup and resembles a water dipper with a small wire handle. They are great for drinking water out of mountain springs, using as a bowl or tea cup (I don't drink coffee), and can be used to boil water or heat food.
     Randal and I used to go hiking up near Comer's Rock in the Mount Rogers National Recreation Area and the views of both Wythe and Grayson counties were breathtaking. The first time I ever saw a real altimeter he had carried one with us to the top of the mountain, it was analog and looked like a large silver pocket watch. We also hiked the New River Trail while it was being established as a state park. We almost always carried trash bags with us and picked up trash along the way. The Norfolk Southern

Railway had donated their old abandoned rail line along the New River to the commonwealth in 1986 and it took some cleanup and improvement to make it suitable as a state park. I am looking forward to taking Wyatt on a hike across some of the old railroad bridges and through the tunnels when he gets older.

    Randal also introduced me to the Appalachian Mountain Dulcimer, the first time I ever saw or heard one played was in his living room. My mother inspired me to learn the guitar and my father inspired me to learn the banjo, but it was Randal who inspired me to play the dulcimer. The unique sound is practically hypnotic when played, a lot like a mandolin, but not quite as harsh. The two instruments I will always cherish and hopefully pass on to my son are my mountain dulcimer made completely out of cedar, and, after I inherit it, my great great grandfather Grover Grubb's banjo.

Chapter 24

When Deer Attack!

Hunting just east of a grove of walnut trees at NORVA Rod & Gun Club, behind the backstop of our 200 yard range, I waited for a deer that I had previously seen twice before and had actually missed once. Around 8 o'clock in the morning she showed up again. Having already setup my shot I patiently waited for her to take the same path as before, across the south ridge and then slowly turning north as she followed a spur in the terrain. She walked past the two trees where I had missed her a few weeks before and presented a nice broadside shot about 75 yards away as she walked. I raised my rifle, the same .308 I used to take my buffalo the previous year, and squeezed off a round. She stumbled and then ran over the spur out of sight!

    I waited the prerequisite 20 minutes to allow the deer to pass on in peace and then lowered my unloaded rifle to the ground with a haul line, adjusted my safety strap, and climbed down out of the tree stand. I found the blood trail and followed it a couple hundred yards when the doe jumped up and ran out of sight again. I noted where she disappeared, reloaded my rifle, placed it on safe, waited another 10 minutes, and more cautiously started stalking the deer. A small puddle of blood and hair had pooled where the deer had lain down, but after that the trail became harder to track. I made my way towards where she had disappeared and spent the next hour tracking her another hundred yards.

Reaching a clear cut area on the edge of the club's property I became concerned the doe would get away by crossing onto someone else's land, so I jumped up on a large tree stump in a slightly elevated area to look around. As I placed my second foot on top of the stump a monster raised up about seven feet in front of me frantically waiving its arms in the air and screaming, "Eeeeeehhhhhhh!" Then I realized the monster was really my deer, raised my rifle to my shoulder, and slapped the trigger. The doe dropped back down and did not move again. I checked my pants to make sure they were still dry and clean, unloaded my rifle, and jumped down beside the deer. Adrenaline pumping, I field dressed it and started making my way back to the lodge.

Chapter 25

Sailing on the Potomac River

Staring up at the blue sky over the port side of the boat with the back of my head slamming into the water of the Potomac River it took all my energy to hold on to the boom and keep myself from falling out of the boat into the muddy water. The young college guy at the helm could barely stay on the boat himself and had no real purpose at this point because the rudder was probably completely out of the water. The older French lady working the jib sheet had a panicked look on her face as I continued to yell out a single command, "Release the jib sheet! Release the jib sheet!" The sailing instructor finally saved us from flipping the 19' Flying Scott sailboat completely over by straddling the distance between the port gunwale and the boom and reaching over to unhook the jib sail from a cleat on the mast where it had gotten hung up. The jib finally blew free, releasing the wind that was over powering the boat and we suddenly swung back into an upright position. The instructor did some quick dancing to avoid going into the drink and wound up kneeling on the bow of the boat as it righted. Similar problems had plagued us earlier that day as we sailed around the small peninsula containing Reagan National Airport, if we didn't tack the jib sheet fast enough it would get hung up on a badly placed cleat and begin to backfill. What had done us in that time was an intensely powerful and sustained gust of wind.

    A similar incident occurred the previous year when I took my first sailing class, but that time a young college student had cleated the main sheet and stopped paying attention as we suddenly had a significant gust of wind. Water started pouring over the port side and the instructor was way up in the bow of the boat, so I had to yank the main sheet out of the kid's hand and uncleat it to keep us from flipping the boat. I felt a little bad about the situation afterwards because he lost his footing and ended up falling into the bottom of the boat as it righted. However, that's better than all of us going for a swim.

Seeing the President's helicopter, Marine One, tops my list of most interesting things that happened while sailing the upper Potomac. Our sailboat received a lot of attention from local law enforcement that day. It all started with a police boat that came towards us and then circled us a few times while we were near Bolling Air Force Base. Within an hour, two police jet skis approached us and circled in close multiple times while the officers looked into our boat. They departed without ever saying a word. A little while after the jet skis left a Huey helicopter flew in and circled us a couple times with the door open and a machine gunner looking down at us. Finally, it all came together and made sense when we saw a formation of whitehawk helicopters, one of which obviously had the President on it.

After obtaining my certification as a small sailboat skipper I started renting sailboats from the Washington Sailing Marina, which is along the upper Potomac between the District of Columbia and Alexandria, Virginia. I eventually bought a small sailing dingy for myself, but it only lasted one season because it was uncomfortable and I ended up flipping it twice. Smaller sailboats are much more susceptible to winds and are harder to control. I upgraded to a Micro Cruiser, with a small cuddy cabin, designed for overnight and weekend sailing on the Great Lakes. It has been a great boat and I have not flipped it. Amy started sailing with me as my confidence with the new boat increased. After a couple summers of sailing the upper Potomac I felt comfortable enough to take the sailboat down to our place on the lower Potomac, where the river empties into the Chesapeake Bay.

The winds and currents are strong where the Potomac and Chesapeake meet, so I started sailing by myself with only a reefed mainsail. I eventually added a storm jib and gradually increased the amount of sail available to catch the wind. Once I became comfortable with the boat and the area I took Amy on a short sail and even took our 3 year old son Wyatt and his cousins out for their first sail. One of them asked, "Is this as fast as it can go?" Kids just don't understand the satisfaction and value of not being in a hurry, working the sails yourself, not having to listen to the whine of a gasoline engine, or comprehend that at over $3.30 per gallon, the gas mileage on a sailboat is awesome!

Photo 10: Sailing my micro-cruiser with my sister Annie.

Growing up in the mountains of Old Dominion limited my exposure to the joys of life on the Chesapeake Bay, but my wife changed all of that. Amy grew up spending most of her summers on the lower Potomac and feels just as strongly about her family traditions on the water as I do about mine in the mountains. So, it should not surprise you that we actually do some crabbing from the deck of our sailboat. It may sound a little strange at first, but what do think people did before they had gas motors? They either rowed or sailed their crab boats; plus my sailboat does have a small motor, but only for emergencies. Crabbing is a lot of fun; it's like fishing, but without all the waiting around doing nothing.

The first time we went crabbing Amy had to teach me everything. What little knowledge I had about crabbing I learned from a reality TV show named Deadliest Catch which filmed commercial crabbing in the Bering Sea off the cost of Alaska; and while you may be able to squint your eyes enough to catch a faint resemblance between my small sailboat and the Northwestern, I am definitely no Sig Hansen! Amy baited the crab pots with fish before leaving the dock and we stacked the pots between us. She even told me that baiting the pots would be my job next time, but I just smiled realizing that I could eventually delegate that responsibility to Wyatt! I piloted the boat out towards the channel of our creek until Amy said stop. She had me hoist a crab pot over the side of the boat and she threw out the buoy. Once we had all the pots soaking we headed back to the dock, and went about our normal daily activities.

Later that afternoon we took the boat back out to check the crab pots, and one of Wyatt's cousins went with us. I would pilot the boat alongside one of the buoys, Amy would hook its line, and she would start hauling up the crab pot. We caught about 3 or 4 crabs in each pot that day and I originally tried to pull them out of the pot with a large set of tongs, which proved rather challenging to do. However, with Amy's guidance I finally just started shaking the crabs out of the pots. The shaking worked out really well until a few crabs fell out onto the deck. Let me tell you something funny, kids with flip flops on their feet suddenly quit worrying about how fast a sailboat can go when angry crabs are flopping around on the deck!

Chapter 26

Naming My Son Wyatt

Amy and I struggled to come up with a great name for our son. We bought baby naming books, evaluated all the names of our fathers, grandfathers, and great grandfathers but could not come up with anything that felt right. I had barely escaped the moniker of Estle Edward Atwell, III when my mother and father named me so I was hesitant to name him David Adam Atwell, Jr. even though the thought of naming him after me really sounded awesome! The one thing I knew for sure was that I did not want to use any of the popular cowboy names, such as Wyatt, that had gained popularity in the 1990s when multiple mainstream movies came out about Wyatt Earp's life.

At the time I shot in a skeet league every Thursday night with a group of guys at Fairfax Rod & Gun Club. We had a lot of fun shooting together and even went duck hunting on the eastern shore once. Unfortunately, I had gotten into a bad habit of breaking both clay targets with one shot when shooting doubles from stations 2 and 6. The rules of skeet specifically indicate you can only break one bird per shot and if you break two they don't count and you have to do it again. The official terminology is shooting "Proof Doubles". Anyway, while it constantly annoyed me that I had to shoot again to prove I could really break the birds separately with two shots, the guys considered it a trick shot and started calling me Wyatt Earp! After a few weeks of the guys calling me Wyatt Earp I had a change of heart and decided I wanted to name my son Wyatt. Amy didn't put up much of a fight because she had liked the name all along and really liked the new story. So, we agreed to name our son Wyatt. Now we just needed to come up with a middle name.

My father had a heart attack about this time and ended up at cardiac center in Salem, Virginia. He eventually recovered, but while dad had some tests one day my sister, Annie, and I decided to take a ride around Salem and tried to relax. We started talking about names and Annie jokingly started reading the street names out loud as we went through intersections. When she said, "Tristan", it hit me like a lightning bolt. Tristan was one of King Arthur's Knights of the Round Table; plus Queen Elizabeth, Virginia's namesake, had a member of her privy council named Tristan; and I knew Amy would love it. I immediately called Amy on my mobile phone and shared the name with her and she did indeed like it. I jokingly asked her if it was because of Brad Pitt's character in the movie "Legends of the Fall" because she had a copy of the movie poster hanging in her house when we started dating. Amy denied it saying she had already thought of that name and indicated I had been the one who didn't liked it. I've never admitted this until now, but one of the reasons I like the name is because of Brad Pitt's character in "Legends of the Fall".

Wyatt and I had the fortuitous opportunity to meet the Commandant of the Marine Corps, General James F. Amos, at Fairfax Rod & Gun Club one day when Wyatt was only 2 years old. I responded sharply with, "Wyatt Tristan Atwell, sir!" when the Commandant asked about my son's name and the Commandant looked Wyatt right in the eyes and said; "Wyatt Tristan Atwell, now that sounds like a President's name." and shook both our hands!

Chapter 27

Where are the Bear Hunting Stories?

At this point you may be wondering about bears; well the answer is simple. My family doesn't bear hunt. In Wythe County where I grew up the Virginia Department of Game and Inland Fisheries (VDGIF) restricted bear hunting to only the lands north of I-81 for years and only recently allowed bear hunting south of I-81. The family farm lies north of I-81, but I never saw a bear or bear sign at the farm. Some of our Musser cousins bear hunted a lot, had bear dogs, and even took trips to Canada to go bear hunting. They gave us a bear roast once and it tasted good, but was a little stringy and greasy.

One time I asked by father why we never went bear hunting and he answered me with a simple question, "How many bear have you ever saw in the woods?" I honestly responded with the number two. He nodded and then asked another question, "Why on earth would you want to hunt an animal so rare that in your entire life you have only seen two of them in the wild?" He made his point and the thought of hunting black bears in Virginia never seriously crossed my mind again. However, one day I may eventually go on a bear hunt, but it would have to be in Alaska. Since then the number of bears I've seen in Virginia has increased from 2 to 4. Both of the new ones were south of I-81 near the dam of Rural Retreat Lake, one crossing a field in broad day light and the other running alongside the road uphill towards the Rural Retreat water towers at night.

David Adam Atwell

My son Wyatt became intrigued by bears the summer he turned three years old while taking a drive along Skyline Drive between Harrisonburg and Front Royal, Virginia. We stopped at one of the camp stores for a snack and he found a display of stuffed black bears in the gift shop. Wyatt wanted the biggest one they had, which was lying on a branch about four feet over his head. Remembering how much my sister loved her stuffed bear named Charlie and I loved my stuffed bear named Teddy as kids I decided to let Wyatt have a bear, but talked him into taking a smaller black bear that you could actually carry around with him. He has slept with that bear every night for almost two years now. He named the bear Bearrie, and you can image our surprise when Wyatt announced to me and his mother that Bearrie was a girl bear. He also told us that Bearrie scares away his bad dreams.

* * * * *

Bearrie the Bear

Bearrie the Bear has a friend named Wyatt,
Who sometimes has bad dreams at night,
But now he sleeps all night long and is quiet,
Because Bearrie protects him from his fright.

Chapter 28

GPS, Land, & Celestial Navigation

Navigating your way around the world has changed dramatically over the years and I have always taken pride in being able to navigate almost anywhere with a quality map and compass. However, taking up sailing posed a new challenge for me, Celestial Navigation. Traveling across land provides adequate landmarks for orienting your map, but when you are on the open water identifiable landmarks are not always available for orienting your chart and identifying your current location. Before the advent of the modern Global Positioning System (GPS) you had to also know how to use a Sextant or Quadrant with the North Star or the noon time sun to properly identify your current latitude on a chart and then sail towards your destination; assuming of course that you know the latitude of your destination, roughly know your current longitudinal location, and are able to ascertain from your chart and compass which direction to go. Determining your precise longitude is even harder than finding your latitude, but isn't always necessary as long as you don't need to be too accurate and are willing to do a little extra sailing.

GPS devices and modern charts and maps are accurate to within just a few feet and allow direct navigation from point to point, but old fashioned navigation with a sextant or quadrant and hand drawn maps required that you first travel to a known latitude and then follow that imaginary line until you reached your destination. This is definitely the long way around, plus measurements must be taken daily and adjustments have to be made often. If you are just one degree off you can miss your destination by as much as 69 miles (the actual distance of 1 degree on the Earth's surface). The fact that you can only see 3 to 150 miles in any direction due to the curvature of the Earth means that you could sail or walk right past your destination without ever seeing it; especially, if your navigation skills are lacking. The actual distance you can see depends on the weather, how high you are above the earth's surface, and the height of your landmark. For example, you can only see a sandbar or grove of trees from a few miles away but a mountain top that is over 2 miles (10,560 feet) higher than the observer can be seen from a hundred miles away or more.

To expand on all this let's start with some simple land navigation that most people are familiar with these days, a cross country family road trip. A typical family traveling from Manassas, Virginia to St. Louis, Missouri would need to plan for a 840 mile trip, 14 hours of actual road time, and 2 full days of traveling in their car or truck. Depending upon the weather, road conditions, and how long it takes to cross the Appalachian Mountains the family would probably need to stay the night in either Charleston, West Virginia; Lexington, Kentucky; or most likely Louisville, Kentucky. To prepare for the trip, the driver would probably either 1) type their destination into the vehicle's GPS device and just drive along until a voice command directs him to take an upcoming turn; or 2) review an interstate road map and follow this easy to remember route.

1. Take I-66 West to I-81 South

2. Take I-81 South to I-64 West

3. Take I-64 West to St. Louis

Quite Simple! However, in the early 19th century two men named Lewis and Clark had to take a completely different route to St. Louis as they led the "Corps of Discovery" across the country on an epic expedition through the northwest Rockies. That journey, interestingly enough, started in Virginia about 85 miles south of Manassas! In preparation for his journey Meriwether Lewis started in Charlottesville, Virginia, travelled to Washington, D.C., and then to Philadelphia, Pennsylvania. Commander Lewis then made his way back down to the Potomac River at Harpers Ferry, Virginia (West Virginia did not exist at the time) and turned northwest towards Pittsburgh, Pennsylvania. When he arrived in Pittsburgh, Lewis commissioned the building of a large keel boat. Keep in mind that he most likely travelled all this distance on horseback, but also could have walked, rode in a carriage, or taken a small boat part of the way. At that time roads in the wilderness area were either nonexistent or little more than a game trail, so rivers were considered the superhighways of the day.

    The Ohio River runs nonstop all the way from Pittsburgh to the Mississippi River, just south of St. Louis. So, Commander Lewis took his new keel boat down the Ohio River and picked up William Clark along the way. I am sure that just like our modern family of travelers; they probably stopped in Louisville to stay the night. The entire journey to St. Louis took them about 6 months from the spring of 1803 until late that fall. Maps of the lands east of the Mississippi and compasses were readily available to men of their means and both Lewis and Clark were familiar with navigating by the stars, but they also employed local scouts whenever possible. This was absolutely necessary when they crossed the Mississippi and headed up the Missouri into uncharted territory. Their most famous guide was Sacagawea, a Native American women married to a french trapper who helped guide them from North Dakota to the Pacific Ocean and back again, which took about two years. She did it all while caring for her young son. How's that for a cross country family trip? Two years and they didn't even have any roads, SUVs, cup holders, portable DVD players, iPods, iPhones, or iPads!

    Now, let's say we wanted to travel to St. Louis by land prior to the 20th century and did not want to use rivers. If we left Manassas and tried to ride a horse or walk to St. Louis the quickest route through the wilderness would typically be considered a straight line and that line happens to be the 38th north latitude, commonly referred to as the 38th parallel. If you look closely at a map of the country you will notice that both cities basically have the same latitude, the 38th degree north latitude. Each degree of latitude is 69 miles from the next, which means that with Manassas at 38.75 degrees and St. Louis 38.63 degrees all a person would have to do is travel due west in a straight line and when they reached the Mississippi River they would be within 8 or 9 miles of St. Louis. The problem is that without a GPS a map, compass, and some good landmarks would be needed to navigate the way. Using a Sextant or Quadrant would actually make this journey easier, but the big challenge would be leaving the 38th latitude to find the best passes through the Appalachian Mountains. Once you made it through the mountain passes you would then have to use the north star or noon time sun to find your current latitude and head either northwest or southwest until rejoining the 38th parallel and continue following that imaginary line all the way to St. Louis. However, after arriving at the Mississippi River you would still need to ask a few local people to help guide you towards St. Louis or waste a lot of time wondering up and down the river looking for the city. Luckily, St. Louis happens to be located right where the Missouri River joins the Mississippi River so it's relatively easy to find; which is probably one of the reasons St. Louis is known as the gateway to the west.

    Now let's take another look at celestial navigation on open water. Assuming you need to take an ocean voyage from Manassas, Virginia to the Azores Islands off the coast of mainland Europe, are an accomplished sailor, have a good understanding of the Atlantic currents and trade winds, and the good sense to avoid the hurricane season you could use a sextant or quadrant to navigate your voyage using the following route as easily as a modern family can take interstate highways from Manassas to St. Louis.

1. Take a small boat or canoe down Bull Run River from Manassas to the Occoquan River and then to the Potomac River.

2. Once on the Potomac River switch to a seagoing vessel, sail down to the Chesapeake Bay, and out into the Atlantic Ocean.

3. Use your sextant or quadrant, compass, and a chart to navigate your way northwards back up to the 38th parallel and then head due east on that imaginary line until you reach the Azores Islands. It would be more efficient and safer to also learn how to determine your current longitude and track your eastward progress.

The journey itself would definitely be a lot harder than driving to St. Louis, but after a month or two at sea you would eventually reach the Azores and could reprovision the boat, pick a new destination in Europe, and sail towards it. The good news is that if you happen to navigate poorly and miss the Azores you would eventually end up in either Europe or Africa anyway, as long as you kept sailing eastward. What an amazing coincidence that Manassas, St. Louis, and the Azores all have the same latitude (more or less).

Chapter 29

Makin' Moonshine

My grandfather enjoyed a drink every now and then and also liked to make his own wine and moonshine. I remember my Paw Paw giving me my first sip of beer and always talking about making dandelion wine in the spring. One time I came home from the Army to visit and he was very proud of his new moonshine still. He kept bragging that if the Revenuers came and took it he could go buy a new one at a yard sale for $5.

A statement like that makes me want to know more, so I decided it was time for me to learn to make moonshine. Paw Paw took me to his kitchen and pointed at a crockpot on the counter that had a big metal mixing bowl on top of it and told me he could make about a pint of moonshine a day with that little still. He lifted the metal bowl, which was full of ice water, reached into the crockpot and pulled out a small cereal bowl and poured its contents into a mason jar. He then placed the little bowl back in the crock pot, floating on a yellowish colored soup, and placed the metal bowl back on top.

The soup was actually corn mash which had been fermented in a 5 gallon bucket. The still was quite simple. My grandfather would pour some corn mash in the crockpot, set it to cook between 170 and 200 degrees, and setup the two bowls as I previously described. Since alcohol turns into steam at 171 degrees and water doesn't until 212 degrees the moonshine would evaporate, rise up towards the metal bowl with ice in it, and condense on the metal bowl. The moonshine would then roll down to the bottom of the metal bowl and drip into the cereal bowl floating on top of the mash. For this to work properly it is important to make sure the temperature is right and the two bowls are not touching each other.

If you decide to try it at home you will need to make sure steam is not escaping between the metal bowl and the crockpot; and also make sure you replace the mash whenever all the alcohol has been distilled. My grandfather would just run his index finger across the bottom of the metal bowl when he poured the moonshine into the mason jar and replace the mash whenever the moisture on his finger didn't taste like shine. You will also need a recipe for making mash, so I have included one below.

Ingredients:

    1 five gallon food service bucket
    1 balloon
    3 gallons of water
    2 cans of corn
    1 five pound bag of sugar
    1 packet of yeast

Directions:

1. Clean and sterilize the bucket and balloon.

2. Mix the water, corn, and sugar in the bucket.

3. Add the yeast to the mix.

4. Place the lid on the bucket and open the pouring spout.

5. Stretch the balloon over the pouring spout opening to create an air tight seal.

6. Place the bucket in a cool drive place until the balloon inflates and deflates, probably about 7 days.

7. Distill the moonshine as previously described.

Chapter 30

The Family Truck Tradition

I mentioned a family truck tradition in the prologue, and from the point of view of this book it started when my Uncle Mike accidentally rolled our old grey pickup truck backwards down the north ridge of the farm right into a tree, denting up the rear bumper and tailgate. I remember the incident because my Paw Paw was very upset and that truck was the first truck I ever drove. I couldn't even reach the pedals properly, but my dad and Uncle Mike put the truck in low gear and let me steer it through a hayfield while they stacked square hay bales on the back. I just had to keep the truck between the rows of hay, which proved rather hard to do and resulted in a lot of cursing by my dad and Uncle Mike.

One of our cousins had the bad luck of shooting his truck, not once, but three times in a matter of minutes. He had an opportunity to shoot at a very nice buck one day and laid his rifle across the hood of his truck. Carefully targeting the deer he squeezed off a round and missed, so he reloaded and shot two more times. After missing the deer three times he quit looking through scope and decided to check his rifle. Only then did he realize that while he had a clear view of the deer in his scope the muzzle of the rifle had actually been pointed at a slightly raised area of his truck's hood, which now had three bullet holes in it, all in a straight line, and just a few inches apart. Obviously, the situation was not something he bragged about or tried to show off, but it's hard to hide three bullet holes in the hood of your truck!

Driving up the steep slope of the west side of the farm, just beyond the tobacco field, I saw a nice buck and decided to take a shot. I set the parking brake, threw the truck in neutral, grabbed my rifle, and eased my way over to a fence post for a good rest. I quickly took my shoot, but the deer ran off, and when I walked over to where the deer had been standing I could not find any hair or blood. My Uncle Mike had been sitting in his truck on the east side of the farm near the tree line and started driving over towards me. I decided to walk back to my truck and meet him. As I approached the trucks, now parked side by side, it looked like my Uncle Mike's truck started moving forward again when I suddenly realized my truck was actually rolling backwards!

I watched in horrific slow motion as my truck gained speed and continued to roll backwards down the hill. I started to run after it and cringed as my truck backed over the edge of an 8 foot drop and groaned as it went over the second 8 foot drop. I grunted and clenched my hands as the truck splashed into the creek and slammed into the south ridge, which was practically vertical in that area. I reached the truck, which was miraculously still running, and tried to drive it out of the creek but the tires just spun and the truck would not budge. Later that day we brought some chains back to the farm and Mike helped me pull my truck out of the creek. I got off lucky because nothing really got damaged except my pride. However, the next morning I couldn't move the truck because the water in my brake drums had frozen overnight and locked up the rear wheels. A little hot water solved the problem, but offered another opportunity for everyone to have a laugh at my expense.

By the way, in case you do not know, the emergency brake on vehicles really does not work as well when the vehicle is pointed up hill. I should have placed the truck in park instead of neutral, or to be real honest, I should have never taken that shot. Stories like this are less common in Virginia now due to the introduction of ATVs and a state law forbidding hunting from vehicles; but I am sure there will still be some good truck stories from the next generation too.

Epilogue

You may find it interesting that I originally outlined this book by hand using a notepad and pen and some of the stories came from my field journals, but I actually wrote the entire manuscript on an Apple iPad, predominately using a wireless keyboard. The ability to easily write and edit the manuscript almost anywhere and anytime was critical to the completion of this book. However, I also printed every chapter and mailed them through the U.S. Postal Service to my father who edited them by hand with a pencil and mailed them back to me. Whenever I received a chapter back from my dad I made a big deal about sitting at the dinner table with my son and reading the letters from Wyatt's Paw Paw out loud. Wyatt, who was only 3 year's old at the time, loved it! I have also bound all those original drafts in a leather cover for him to have when he gets older and to share with his own children. Teaching the younger generation the old ways like this helps preserve tradition while also helping prevent history from repeating itself because the next generation will better understand why we do things the way we do. I am sure Wyatt will easily learn all about texting, twitter, facebook, or whatever the latest communications technology is for his generation with very little help from me; but at least he'll also know that all you really need is a voice to speak, pen and paper to write with, or just a stick to draw in the dirt. None of these require the internet, a phone, electricity, or any other modern conveniences.

Writing this book entailed a personal journey of unexpected twists and turns as I decided which adventures and stories needed inclusion. I hope you enjoyed them and also hope that in another 20-30 years I have enough new experiences and the strength to write them down again. I have tried to save enough stories to start the next volume of Appalachian Safari and in closing leave you with the following thoughts and recommendations for the future.

    Embrace and use new technology whenever it improves the quality of your life, but never forget the old ways of doing things. Always learn a low tech way of doing things in case your new technology fails. For example, use a GPS device, but learn to use a map and compass. Buy groceries at the store, but raise some tomato, cucumber, and pepper plants in your backyard or on your balcony; and learn to can your own vegetables. Go to an orchard or farm and pick your own apples, peaches, and strawberries from time to time. You should also try dehydrating your own fruits and vegetables and making your own jerky too. Hunt and fish with modern rifles, shotguns, and fishing tackle, but learn to use muzzleloaders, a bow, traps, and a simple cane fishing pole. Buy clothes at the store, but take time to learn to sew, knit, quilt, and work leather.

    Work hard when there is work to be done and enjoy other endeavors to their fullest potential whenever you have time. Lead from the front and don't be afraid to work side by side with others, even if you have to get your hands dirty. Enjoy solitude but embrace both family and friends. Make your accomplishments known, but be humble. Realize that a quiet professional actually earns more personal satisfaction and respect than a braggart. If you cannot be humble then afford others the pretense of humility, this little piece of advice actually comes from Benjamin Franklin.

    Treat all beings with respect and honor; every man, woman, child, and animal on this earth have the right to succeed or fail on their own terms. Give each individual an opportunity to prove his or her worth. Avoid blinding cultural stereotypes that drive people apart, but do not put yourself, family, or friends at risk until a man or woman has proven their individual character. If someone falters, give them a cautious second chance and a third chance if they deserve it.

Hold individual liberty and freedom above all else in importance, and not just your own. When someone else's individual liberties are infringed you must defend them, otherwise there is nothing to prevent your liberties from also being infringed. The free exchange of ideas, goods, and services are the foundation of liberty itself and must be protected for everyone and from anyone who would restrict them for their own benefit or for the benefit of the government at the expense of individual freedom. Unfortunately, people are often slow to stand up for liberty and sometimes need a leader to stand up first. When necessary, be that leader, but remember that you cannot lead if you have yourself waited too long to take action or if you personally risk too much too quickly. Always remember that your individual rights end at the point where you start to infringe someone else's rights, life, liberty, or pursuit of happiness.

Become an expert marksman, own and maintain a modern service rifle, shotgun, and/or pistol, but remember that violence and deadly force should be used as a tool of last resort to protect only life and liberty. Your mind, common sense, discussion, open debate without the fear of reprisal, and strategy must be your weapons of choice in all battles until backed into a corner with nowhere left to retreat.

Also, one last piece of advice for when you are married; just go ahead and take out the trash, help with the dishes, cook a meal once in a while, and occasionally clean the bathroom. You will ultimately end up doing these things anyway.

Made in the USA
Lexington, KY
26 March 2013